AF726528

The Return of the HBCUs

Origin, Mission, and Economic Mobility

Cedric Grice

innovativeink PUBLISHING
A Division of Kendall Hunt

Cover image Shutterstock.com

innovativeink PUBLISHING
A Division of Kendall Hunt

www.innovativeinkpublishing.com
Send all inquiries to:
4050 Westmark Drive
Dubuque, IA 52004-1840

Print ISBN: 979-8-3851-8892-5
eBook ISBN: 979-8-3851-8893-2

Published in the United States of America

Contents

Acknowledgement

In the tradition of the West African Griots, this book is not solely my story; rather, it reflects my version of the histories and economic concepts shared with me and others by various storytellers over the years. My ability to convey this narrative stems from the unwavering love and support my family has shown me throughout my life. Nonetheless, no story of mine would have ever reached the page if my wife, son, and daughter hadn't taken the time to listen to it first.

Introduction

The main characters of this book are the Historically Black Colleges and Universities (HBCUs), which were buried deep within the federal legislation created to bring to life the Great Society as envisioned by President Lyndon B. Johnson (LBJ) in his speech at the University of Michigan on May 22, 1964. The Great Society legislation bestowed the HBCU title upon certain higher education institutions established before 1964 whose principal mission was to educate Black communities as defined in the 1965 Higher Education Act.

One of the Great Society's priority objectives was to end racial discrimination in the United States, which Enlightenment philosophers baked into the cake of Western European societies' definition of freedom. Racial discrimination, legally practiced before and after the United States' colonial period, is the leading source of most economic and social inequities for Black people living in the United States. The Great Society legislation provided HBCUs and all higher educational institutions with additional funding to address the economic and social inequality caused by the practice of legal racial discrimination.

This practice restricted Black people from participating in established schools, colleges, universities, and labor markets and attempted to stop the development of economically viable Black communities and the creation of generational Black family wealth. However, this practice did not stop the growth of Black institutions specifically designed to provide knowledge to the Black community needed to overcome these obstacles.

The book is unique because it recognizes HBCUs as the true protagonists of this epic tale of how the Black community emerged from a hopeless predicament. However, like most famous stories, the book contains a twist near the end, and the protagonists transform during the journey to become the antagonists.

This book, however, is a factual version of an often-told story about the resilience of the African people who came to America under involuntary servitude and how, after hundreds of years, they renegotiated the terms of their servitude and place in American society. HBCUs, with the support of the Black community, eventually took the lead in delivering these African people out of chattel slavery into independent Black families and communities and finally into full U.S. citizenship.

This book is a cultural story of the Black people forced into involuntary servitude in the Americas and how the hero eventually saved the people, a classic storyline shared by every human culture. The story goes like this: After long years of servitude and despair, the roots of a story take hold among the people, which at first is only a rumor. The rumor is always the same. Under certain conditions and after certain events, the hero will emerge to lead the people to whatever they perceive as freedom, paradise, or, in the case of the previously enslaved Black people of America, the Beloved Community.

One of the most famous students groomed by HBCUs, Dr. Martin Luther King Jr. (MLK), who orchestrated the Montgomery bus boycott, stated that the boycott's purpose was "reconciliation, redemption, and the creation of the beloved community." MLK's concept of the Beloved Community, like LBJ's vision of the Great Society, was based on justice, equal opportunity, and love for one's fellow human beings.

This community could be achieved through nonviolent social change. Everyone would have access to resources and opportunities, eliminating poverty and hunger. Conflicts would be resolved through understanding and cooperation. Aggression, discrimination, and segregation would be eradicated, and all individuals would be treated with dignity and respect.

Therefore, in this book, we look back at what HBCUs did to establish the Black community and how their students implemented the HBCUs' vision to understand if their mission was achieved and, if not, how to navigate a path forward. The book reviews the histories of HBCUs from their inception until now by aggregating HBCU data to reveal the anatomy of a typical HBCU. The data collected for these institutions and their surrounding communities are a quantifiable record of their stories, creating a statistical demographic and financial benchmark for analysis.

The book's first prominent finding is that each HBCU is integral to its surrounding community. Despite the iron gates surrounding the physical boundaries of most HBCU campuses and separating them from the community, the HBCU and the surrounding community are headed in the same economic direction.

Second, HBCUs and the Black communities surrounding HBCUs share a symbiotic bond. The communities support the HBCUs, and in turn, the HBCUs contribute to their development. This bond may waver but remains unbroken, demonstrating the lasting bond, mutual support, and developmental reliance between the two characters of this story.

Third, HBCUs represent the best of the Black community, are the origin of Black culture, and are the link to its African past. HBCUs are the economic engine responsible for the growth of the Black community.

While other works on this subject may cover what, when, and where of HBCU activities over the years, this book takes a different approach. It examines the data collected on the impact of HBCUs' day-to-day activities, quantifying the results to provide valuable insights into the next steps for these institutions' progress and their return to prominence in the economic development of the Black community.

This book offers an iterative process for objectively assessing the status of each HBCU by quantitatively and qualitatively evaluating their performance and making specific recommendations for improvement based on the evaluation findings for each particular HBCU. The evaluation findings and recommendations are the foundation for developing a strategic planning and implementation process for that HBCU. The aim is to provide a comprehensive understanding of how HBCUs impact the economic development of the Black community and offer insights into how economic development activities are linked to their principal mission: the education of the Black community.

What's Up with HBCUs

HBCUs have been getting lots of buzz lately, as if they had recently been invented, which is not the case. These institutions have been imparting knowledge to all who dared to enter their gates for over one hundred and fifty years, and their notoriety has ebbed and flowed during those years.

The student-musicians produced at HBCUs are known across the globe, starting with the Fisk Jubilee Singers, who were the first to bring recognition to their college and the musical capabilities of Black Americans in the early 1900s. Since then, numerous jazz musicians, opera and gospel singers, composers, and performers have matriculated through HBCUs, so the current buzz cannot just be about music.

During the 1960s, 1970s, and 1980s, HBCU student-athletes made headlines at the national level for their contribution to professional championship football and basketball teams and on the international level for their gold medal performances as members of various U.S. Olympic teams. But once again, this new buzz cannot just be about athletic ability.

Many A-list celebrities are generating this buzz by recognizing HBCUs and incorporating them into their work. These celebrities include Beyonce and J-Z, Chris Paul III, Stephen A. Smith, Deion "Prime Time" Sanders, Shaquille O'Neal, Master P, Oprah Winfrey, Spike Lee, Denzel Washington, MacKenzie Scott, and Terrence J. These celebrities speak on behalf, act in support, partner with, and give financial contributions directly to HBCUs.

So, what did HBCUs do lately to suddenly garner all this attention and support?

Dr. Jelani M. Favors, the Henry E. Frye Distinguished Professor of History at North Carolina A&T State University, gives an excellent explanation of what HBCUs did to create all this buzz in his book *Shelter in a Time of Storm: How Black Colleges Fostered Generations of Leadership and Activism*, published in 2019. This book emphasizes the often-overlooked role HBCUs played in obtaining the freedom and prosperity that the Black community enjoys today.

Historically, HBCUs are the pillars that support the Black experience in America since they were established during and after the Reconstruction era of the nineteenth century. The Reconstruction era, which followed the Civil War, led to several significant social and political changes in the United States. HBCUs are a direct product of this era, created to transition slave laborers into free laborers and to establish the free Black communities.

Today, the yearly rituals of HBCU campus homecomings are celebrated, and they are full of cultural pageantry associated with high-stepping bands, fraternities, and sorority step shows. However, it is essential to recognize that their role in producing social movements and reshaping the contours of American democracy is equally significant and worthy of appreciation.

The five specific ways in which HBCUs have directly impacted the Black culture of America is in their response to the end of Reconstruction, the creation of Black leadership, their role in the New Negro Movement and the Harlem Renaissance, their contribution to the Modern Civil Rights Movement, and their continued influence in the present day.

Stepping Up After Reconstruction

Reconstruction (1865-1877) was a political reward for the assistance the Black population provided the North in defeating the Confederacy and winning back the states that seceded from the Union. The most important part of the reward was the Reconstruction Amendments to the Constitution, which ended slavery and granted citizenship and equal protection under the law for the previously enslaved Black population.

However, the most visible and valuable reward was the protection the ten Black Army regiments, the United States Colored Troops (USCT), provided. Under the leadership of white officers, these regiments were assigned to the five military districts in which the southern states were divided during Reconstruction.

This protection lasted until it became part of a political deal by the Republican Party to elect Rutherford B. Hayes president in 1876 in a close election that had to be decided by a vote of the House of Representatives. In exchange for the presidency, the Republican Party agreed to support the reassignment of the Black regiments stationed in the South to protect the settlement of the Western territories against Native American resistance.

This political deal made HBCUs invaluable, and the sole American institution dedicated to guiding the Black population of 4 million people on the journey from slavery to freedom. HBCUs served as "shelters in a time of storm" as racial violence and domestic terrorism became normalized and etched into the fabric of the South and the nation after Reconstruction.

HBCUs created an enclave that blunted those effects and provided Black youth with a space where their human dignity went unquestioned, and they could develop the tools and skills needed for the struggles ahead. HBCUs would serve as laboratories of dissent by stimulating race consciousness and equipping Black youth with the intellectual abilities to counter and deconstruct white supremacy.

Providing the Leadership for the Black Community

The Reconstruction umbrella of protection provided by the Black Army regiments was not impervious to attacks of violence designed to impede the progress of the newly freed Black population in the South. So, as the HBCUs entered the post-Reconstruction period, they were required to create a leadership development program for the Black community that could strategically combat violent attacks against their efforts to lead the Black community toward racial equality in the twentieth century.

The connection between the white HBCU leadership, American missionaries, and Industrial philanthropists allowed the work of HBCUs to continue to spread into all eleven states of the defeated Confederacy despite violent opposition. The dominant principle underpinning the HBCU experience was student training that fostered racial responsibility and service to the Black community as the HBCUs worked to refine and upgrade their curriculum to earn and maintain accreditation.

HBCUs trained future leaders who were empowered by the humanities and social sciences. These academic fields trained students to think critically about the human condition and transform their communities by embracing race consciousness that covertly refuted white supremacy and adopting cultural nationalist impulses.

The latter created generations of "race men" and "race women" who created and sustained Black organizations, businesses, and institutions. This resulted in a generation of Black leaders emerging from HBCUs who used talents developed in these crucial spaces to champion the causes of Black liberation. Numerous leaders, including Anna Julia Cooper, W.E.B. Du Bois, Ida B. Wells, and James Weldon Johnson, were transformed by their training at HBCUs and played critical roles in shaping the early civil rights movement.

Creating a Black Culture

The violence white post-World War I reaction to the advancements achieved by the success of Black leadership resonated on HBCU campuses in what became known as the New Negro Movement. The vital lecture circuit that placed the nation's foremost scholars, activists, and organizers in proximity with idealistic youth studying at HBCUs was critical to this development.

Furthermore, HBCUs played critical roles in reasserting and redefining the Black aesthetic in what became known as the Harlem Renaissance. The artistic expressions of HBCU alums such as Zora Neale Hurston and Langston Hughes helped to define the era, enriching our cultural heritage. In contrast, Black college faculty such as Aaron Douglas, Lois Mailou Jones, and Hale Woodruff, who were significant artists, cultivated the creative energies of students who challenged white supremacy through art, inspiring a new generation of artists and thinkers.

Winning the Struggle Against the Legal Practice of Racial Discrimination

Post-World War II militancy found its way to HBCU campuses as scores of Black World War II veterans, with a broader worldview, returned to HBCUs, which carved out space for the intensifying radicalism that enveloped Black students. HBCUs served as epicenters of this growing dissent, as students and HBCU alums, such as Ella Baker, Thurgood Marshall, and Dr. Martin Luther King Jr., played significant roles in publicly challenging the practice of racial discrimination.

Starting with the *Brown v. Board of Education*, a Supreme Court Case in 1954, HBCU-trained students across the South began to adopt an aggressive strategy of direct action against the legal practice of racial discrimination. Black students were ready to wade through deep psychological rivers of fear that had immobilized earlier generations.

In doing so, they sought public fights that vaulted the struggle against racial discrimination to the front pages of newspapers and led off the story of national television news. They also birthed critical civil rights organizations, formed of students from HBCUs, including the Student Nonviolent Coordinating Committee, the Congress for Racial Equality, and the Southern Christian Leadership Council.

Representing the Best of the Black Community

HBCUs continued to serve as vital nerve centers for movement activity through the late 1960s and 1970s. HBCUs cultivated and embraced the Black Power Movement. However, student radicalism was increasingly suppressed in this era as HBCUs fell victim to violence from Army National Guard Units and local law enforcement. Students were killed on the campuses of South Carolina State University, North Carolina A&T State University, Jackson State University, and Southern University.

Nevertheless, these institutions have remained at the forefront of the struggle for Black liberation in America. They are unapologetically pro-Black, providing a platform for Black students to openly celebrate Barack Obama's election as the first Black president of the United States and a space to share their outrage during the spring of 2020 when the world witnessed what police oppression against Black people looks like by watching George Floyd's death.

Their role in the Black Liberation Movement is a source of inspiration and empowerment. Still, more importantly, HBCUs were the source of the knowledge needed to engage in the struggle effectively. The newly discovered knowledge of the role of HBCUs in the fight for freedom is causing all the buzz.

The new knowledge about HBCUs does not stop with a better understanding of their role in the struggle but should extend to include a sense of how HBCUs led in the establishment of the first free Black communities. In the words of jazz musician Miles Davis (whose father was an HBCU graduate of the University of Arkansas at Pine Bluff), knowledge is freedom, and ignorance is slavery. More knowledge about the role HBCUs played in establishing the Black community will lead to a better Black community.

This book tells the story of why HBCUs are worthy of the support and recognition they seem to be suddenly receiving. HBCUs were the catalysts that brought together the tools and skills the people of African descent needed to renegotiate their terms of servitude and their place in American society.

The Return of the HBCUs is the story of how these institutions can continue educating the Black community and return to completing the construction of the Beloved Community as envisioned by so many HBCU students whose lives were dedicated to and sacrificed for that purpose.

CHAPTER 1

Knowledge is Freedom

1.1 Enlightenment Freedom

In 1865, 4 million Black people of African descent finished participating in the first hundred-plus years of a democratic experiment created in 1776 by English colonial revolutionaries in America. This experiment furnished the English colonial revolutionaries with financial independence and fundamental human rights based on democratic principles established by European philosophers during the Age of Enlightenment.

However, the same financial independence and fundamental human rights were not extended to the English colonialists of African descent unless they could prove they or their ancestors fought in the American Revolutionary War. While the Age of Enlightenment advocated financial independence and human rights, the economic imperatives of the era justified and perpetuated slavery.

The application of Enlightenment principles routinely included the practice of racial discrimination regarding enslaved Africans and other marginalized groups. Therefore, to achieve financial independence and fundamental human rights, these 4 million Black people needed to defeat the legal practice of racial discrimination contained in the foundational legal documents and laws developed by the American colonial revolutionaries that created the democratic experiment.

To carry out this task, HBCUs built an educational network that distributed the knowledge needed to produce Black college students who became nonviolent revolutionaries. These students developed the skills to use the foundational legal documents and laws the American colonial revolutionaries developed to defeat the legal practice of racial discrimination, gain economic independence, and create free Black communities.

The Declaration of Independence and the U.S. Constitution contained many progressive and controversial democratic principles. Enlightenment philosophers like John Locke postulated that individuals have inherent rights to life, liberty, and property, principles prominently reflected in the Declaration of Independence. Additionally, Montesquieu's advocacy for separating government powers to avert any singular branch from gaining excessive authority significantly shaped the structure of the U.S. government, as shown in the first three articles of the U.S. Constitution.

The Enlightenment period coincided with the development of the English colonies in America, thereby influencing the thoughts of America's founding fathers as they began to craft the founding documents declaring their freedom and economic independence from England. Enlightened ideas emphasized reason, science, individualism, and democratic principles over tradition and religious authority as a way of governing society.

Central to the Enlightenment is the notion that government is a contract between the governed and their rulers. This ideology emphasizes the populace's right to dismantle a government that fails to safeguard its rights. This framework contributed to the American Revolution. These ideas replaced religious authority with majority rule, advocated violent revolution as an acceptable means of achieving an agreement between the government and the governed, and replaced divine rights with political compromise to share power.

The Enlightenment strongly emphasized reason, scientific inquiry, and empirical data as foundations for knowledge and decision making, paving the way for advancements in various scientific and technological domains. This intellectual movement promoted a culture of inquiry and innovation while underscoring the importance of individual rights and the belief in human progress and self-improvement—values that became integral to American society.

However, despite the Enlightenment's promotion of liberty and equality, many proponents held conflicting views about race. The emphasis on reason and science also eased the emergence of scientific racism, wherein confident Enlightenment thinkers employed pseudoscientific methodologies to validate racial hierarchies and the subjugation of non-European populations.

Therefore, the application of Enlightenment principles routinely included the practice of racial discrimination regarding enslaved Africans and other marginalized groups. Furthermore, Enlightenment notions concerning progress and civilization were employed to rationalize European colonialism and the exploitation of non-European societies, thereby contributing to the proliferation of racial discrimination and the establishment of racial hierarchies.

The Age of Enlightenment left a dual legacy; it laid the foundation for democratic ideals and human rights while easing the development and justification of racial discrimination and colonial exploitation. The U.S. Constitution advocated racial discrimination, a hierarchical view of human differences that emphasized European superiority or a white-over-Black ideology. Suffice it to say, the practice of racism was baked into the cake of the Enlightenment's concept of freedom, and the freedom the U.S. government provided to its citizens.

The Three-Fifths Compromise used this Enlightenment ideology to unite the thirteen separate colonial states into one indivisible nation after the successful revolution provided freedom from the English government. This compromise provided a means for sharing political power between the Northern and Southern states despite their differences regarding freedom, economic independence, and the use of free and enslaved labor.

Located in Article I, Section 2, Clause 3 of the U.S. Constitution, this compromise officially established an inferior class of citizenship based on racial discrimination. This clause upheld the democratic principle that all people are created equal. Still, it allowed the legal practice of racial discrimination by valuing a person as less than a person based exclusively on racial differences.

While Enlightenment ideals were quickly transferred into legal documents and laws, changing society's actions to match these laws took centuries. Therefore, contradictions between actions and laws existed for many years between the colonialists and the Black people trapped in the democratic experiment that the colonists created.

The Declaration of Independence advocated violent revolution as an acceptable solution for the governed to remove themselves from the government when the government applied the law discriminatorily. This solution was used to resolve the intractable differences between the Northern and Southern states about the supremacy of state rights over federal authority, the equality of all people under the law, free versus slave labor, and the legal practice of racial discrimination.

To resolve these controversies, the Southern states declared their independence from the United States of America. This act of rebellion to form a separate nation was the leading cause of the Civil War.

While the Southern states acted within their rights, they violated the Treaty of Paris between England and the United States. The treaty gave the English territory in North America to the United States and not to each state's colonial governmental body. Therefore, the war was fought over who owned the land, the states or the United States.

After the war, the flow of resources from the North to rebuild the South funded the establishment of HBCUs. These were the only institutions with a mandate to restore the lives of the people who were explicitly damaged by the three-fifths compromise and its inherent support of racial discrimination.

The HBCUs built an educational network that distributed knowledge to college students who would use the laws of the founding fathers to legally declare their right to attack the government's discriminatory application of the law. These HBCU nonviolent student revolutionaries eventually developed the skills necessary to defeat the legal practice of racial discrimination and gain political and economic freedom for Black communities.

The student's main aim was to demonstrate how the freedom earned by Black participation in the Civil War was being violated by the legal practice of racial discrimination at the state and local levels due to the lack of enforcement at the federal level. The education HBCUs bestow upon their students provides the knowledge required and the courage to practice human civil rights instead of tolerating the practice of racial discrimination in the United States and the world.

One hundred years after the end of the Civil War in 1865, HBCU students appeared as the leaders of a nonviolent revolution, famously known as the Civil Rights Movement. Forty-one years from now, we will celebrate two of the most meaningful events in the development of American democracy: the 200th anniversary of the end of the U.S. Civil War in 1865 and the 100th anniversary of the signing of the Voter Rights Act of 1965 that ended the legal practice of racial discrimination.

This is also the 100th anniversary of the HBCU student nonviolent revolution, which exposed the violence and human suffering caused by racial discrimination in the United States and the world. It is our responsibility to ensure that HBCUs, the institutions that sheltered and honed the skills of the nonviolent student revolutionaries, survive to preserve an environment where these skills can continue to be learned and celebrated at future anniversaries centuries from now.

1.2 Runaway Freedom

Leaving the Old World for the New World in the fifteenth century required a set of official documents, just as a set of official documents is part of the immigration process of the twenty-first century. Every immigrant's arrival in the New World was accompanied by documentation recording whether the immigrant arrived voluntarily or involuntarily and the terms of their freedom.

Before the start of the American Civil War, obtaining documentation of freedom for an enslaved Black person was not impossible, but official documents to verify one's liberty or ownership were required. The methods of obtaining these documents were limited; to get the documents verifying freedom, the owner of the enslaved person must grant freedom to the enslaved person on or before the owner's death or sell the proof of ownership to another buyer.

The only other viable option for freedom involved the enslaved person finding a way to escape ownership and settling in the nearest state that allowed Black people to live freely without proper documentation. The states that did not require papers verifying your freedom were above the Mason–Dixon line.

The Mason–Dixon line separates Pennsylvania, Maryland, Delaware, and West Virginia and was named after the surveyors Charles Mason and Jeremiah Dixon, who surveyed between 1763 and 1767. It became symbolic as the dividing line between the Northern free states and the Southern slave states, both in a literal and figurative sense.

The states above the Mason–Dixon line were tolerant of Black people living freely within their communities without the need to produce official documents verifying the origins of their freedom. The line represented the geographical boundary, the cultural, political, and social divide between the North and South during the Civil War, and the fight against racial discrimination.

The start of the Civil War shifted the Mason–Dixon line to any point behind the Union Army lines because the Union Army did not require the Black men, women, and children who sought refuge behind its lines to present any papers verifying the origins of their freedom. The Union Army's humanitarian reaction to the enslaved Black people set in motion five historic actions leading to freedom for the Black community.

These actions, listed in the order of their occurrence, are (1) an end to the economic benefits of the practice of chattel slavery in the United States, (2) the issuance of Presidential Executive Order Proclamation 95 (the Emancipation Proclamation), (3) the passage of the 13th Amendment of the United States Constitution, which ended the legal practice of slave labor in the United States, (4) the end of the Civil War and (5) and the most important of the actions, the development of HBCUs.

This unofficial response, which began with the hostilities in 1861, is a testament to the resilience and determination of the Black enslaved families and a demonstration of American opposition to slavery. The enslaved population's response to the presence of the Union Army, despite their understanding of the permanence of their enslavement, was a powerful demonstration of their desire for freedom and self-determination.

The uncoordinated response of army commanders in Union-controlled Confederate territory was a beacon of hope in a time of great uncertainty. The response included setting up camps behind Union lines, which instantly provided Black families freedom without any of the required documentation.

In addition, the Army provided shelter, food, and clothing needed to stay alive, previously only offered by their enslavers on the plantation. This response created an alternative that increased the financial risk associated with business transactions dependent upon the permanency of ownership assumed in the practice of chattel slavery.

Union Army Major General Benjamin Butler is credited with coining the term "contraband camp" to describe the camps of self-emancipated Black people set up behind Union Army lines under the supervision of the Army and with help from missionaries. Contraband is a military term used to describe material, supplies, and equipment captured from an opposing military force.

Once captured, these items were not returned to the opposing force, and the Union Army used this argument in response to Southern claims for the return of enslaved people under the Fugitive Slave Act of 1850 during the war. The act required that all escaped enslaved people be returned to enslavement upon capture and required all government officials and citizens of free states to cooperate with the enforcement of this law.

The Union Army's unofficial response originated with the actions of three men—Frank Baker, Shepard Mallory, and James Townsend—who were enslaved field hands on a farm near Hampton, Virginia. Following the first gunfire of the Civil War at Fort Sumter on April 12, 1861, their master took the three men to Sewell's Point, close to present-day Norfolk, Virginia, where they were assigned to construct an artillery battery for the Confederacy.

While laboring at the Confederate outpost in Norfolk, these men discovered their owner's plans to transfer them to North Carolina, where they would serve in the construction of another rebel installation. Instead of facing permanent separation from their families, the men chose to undertake a dangerous escape toward freedom by heading to the Union stronghold at Fort Monroe in Virginia near Norfolk.

Baker, Mallory, and Townsend knew the harsh consequences of escaping and the jeopardy their families in Hampton, Virginia, were placed in due to their actions. They did not realize that the impact of their choice would become a pivotal moment in the Civil War, long before the battles of Vicksburg and Gettysburg occurred.

The three men escaped, rowing a small boat across Hampton Roads to Fort Monroe, one of the few Union-controlled locations in the South. The fort's commander, General Benjamin Butler, recognized the illogical nature of adhering to the Fugitive Slave Law, which mandated that he return the three runaways to their master to continue constructing a Confederate battery that posed a threat to his fort.

Union policy on slavery was explicit: President Abraham Lincoln had consistently stated from the start of hostilities that he did not intend to interfere with the practice of chattel slavery and only sought to suppress the Southern rebellion. Therefore, given that Virginia had seceded from the Union, General Butler argued, he no longer had a constitutional duty to return the runaways.

Instead, following military law governing conflicts between nations, he would classify the three men as contraband property used by the enemy against the Union. The escape of Baker, Mallory, and Townsend and the general's clever maneuver proved significant by allowing President Lincoln to maintain his political position on chattel slavery.

However, when other enslaved Black Americans learned that three men had been granted refuge, they began to escape to Fort Monroe, which they called Freedom's Fortress. By the end of the war, half a million formerly enslaved people and free Black people sought protection behind Union lines.

The effects of the approaching Union Army were the same but more dramatic in Western Tennessee, where many of the area's 275,000 enslaved people abandoned farms and towns in anticipation of the approaching Union Army. In the summer of 1862, as the Army of General Ulysses S. Grant approached Memphis, Tennessee, his Army was surrounded by hungry and poorly clad runaways.

Grant ordered Chaplain John Eaton to requisition surplus tents, blankets, rations, and tools and establish a camp for the runaways, who had been supplying forced labor for the Confederate Army as teamsters, construction laborers, and body servants. Eaton established the first contraband camp at Grand Junction, Tennessee, outside of Memphis, in August 1862, and later that year, Northern missionaries and church leaders arrived to establish schools, administer religious and medical services, and even provide political education.

By March 1863, the Grand Junction Contraband Camp housed 1,713 runaways, and contraband camps stretched throughout the occupied parts of the Mississippi Valley from Memphis to New Orleans. The Army employed the able Freemen, the new name taken by the runaways, at fifty cents per day on abandoned farms, government-supervised plantations, and military projects. Approximately 20,000 male freedmen were inducted into the Union Army as U.S. Colored Troops (USCT). By 1866, USCT regiments comprised 40 percent of the Union army troops raised in Tennessee. The workforce provided by freedmen troops and the contraband camps gave the Union a decided edge in sustaining the occupation in Tennessee and winning the war in the Western theater.

The contraband camps became the foundation for the postwar Black community. They facilitated the rapid urbanization of the formerly enslaved people, most of whom had lived in rural areas. Runaways from the Arkansas delta, western Kentucky, northern Mississippi, and rural West Tennessee flowed into Memphis until freedmen outnumbered whites in 1865.

Filled with log cabins, frame buildings, and often tents with dirt floors, the camps became so large that Northern missionaries and local newspapers frequently named them "New Africa." The large camps on Memphis' southern boundary were Camp Shiloh, Camp Fiske (near Union Fort Pickering), and Camp Dixie (President's Island).

Camp Shiloh had over 300 houses and 2,000 residents, as well as churches, schools, saloons, lunchrooms, and barbershops. The contrabands in Camp Dixie cultivated 300 acres of cotton and built a sawmill and a school in 1863. Missionaries and ministers performed and recorded the first legal marriages for thousands of formerly enslaved people in these camps.

In 1863, the Freedmen's Department of the Army was established under John Eaton to manage the camps. Over one hundred contraband camps were created during the war to provide refuge for enslaved people who ran away to Union-controlled territory. The following are the names of some contraband camps:

- Fort Monroe Contraband Camp—Virginia, Established in 1861
- Hampton Contraband Camp—Virginia, Established in 1861
- Camp Barker—Washington, D.C., Established in 1862

- Grand Junction Contraband Camp—Tennessee, Established in 1862
- Camp Shiloh—Tennessee, Established in 1862
- Camp Fiske—Tennessee, Established in 1862
- Camp Dixie—Tennessee, Established in 1862
- Helena Contraband Camp—Arkansas, Established in 1862
- Corinth Contraband Camp—Mississippi, Established in 1862
- Freedmen's Colony of Roanoke Island—North Carolina, Established in 1863
- Natchez Contraband Camp—Mississippi, Established in 1863
- Vicksburg Contraband Camp—Mississippi, Established in 1863
- Camp Nelson—Kentucky, Established in 1863
- The Bermuda Hundred Contraband Camp—Virginia, Established in 1864

These camps were home to thousands of self-emancipated residents who used them to start their journey toward freedom. The camps empowered these Black people to become members of the free labor market, seek an education, and help with the Union war effort.

On January 1, 1963, President Lincoln issued a presidential executive order, Proclamation 95, better known as the Emancipation Proclamation. President Lincoln finally backed General Butler's decision about the camps because it did not contest the status of the enslaved individuals as property.

This first response in 1861 became the model for the official response, and the executive order provided the legal basis and financial resources for the formerly enslaved Black families "to be received into the armed service of the United States." The proclamation required the executive branch of the federal government, including the Army and the Navy, to "recognize and support the freedom of all those able to flee enslavement" in ten Confederate states

The proclamation provided freedom to 4 million enslaved people able to flee to the nearest Union Army line. At the same time, it deprived the Confederate states of slave labor, the most critical resource supporting their economy and ability to fund their war effort.

The Union Army and Navy could now use these resources to fight against the Confederates by making the self-emancipated Black families eligible for paid military service in the Union Army and Navy. This reversal of economic fortune caused by the presidential executive order was essential to the collapse of the Confederacy's ability to pursue the war effort and explains why the Emancipation Proclamation was mistakenly but often celebrated as the end of slavery and the Civil War.

Gaining freedom from slavery no longer required the enslaved person to buy their freedom or be granted independence from their legal owner. The owner no longer had to provide the person acquiring freedom with proof of ownership and documents showing that the person had acquired freedom by giving some form of consideration to the owner, such as proof of purchase and proof of sale.

Proclamation 95 did not require any documents to be transferred to show proof of ownership or proof of sale. Any enslaved person with the courage or opportunity to seek shelter behind the lines of the approaching Union Army was free.

This type of freedom was not enjoyed by the enslaved people still living in the border states that practiced slavery but remained in the Union. Enslaved people in the border states gained their freedom at different times:

- The District of Columbia abolished slavery on April 16, 1862, with the District of Columbia Compensated Emancipation Act.
- Maryland abolished slavery on November 1, 1864, when the state adopted a new constitution,
- Missouri abolished slavery on January 11, 1865, by an ordinance passed by the state convention
- Kentucky and Delaware abolished slavery with the ratification of the Thirteenth Amendment on December 6, 1865.

Proclamation 95 provided an effective and efficient model for addressing the social, economic, and logistical issues created by giving freedom to 4 million enslaved people. The model provided a temporary solution for transitioning slave labor to free labor by making the Union Army the employer of camp residents and paying them for the work performed on behalf of the Union Army and Navy during the war.

Setting up camps on abandoned plantations or near Union Army camps was an effective and efficient solution to providing services to the Black families whose freedom the Union Army now had to protect and preserve. These camps provided the most convenient means of distributing shelter, food, clothing, and education to the formerly enslaved people in the areas surrounding the camps.

The model aligned perfectly with the resources and skill sets available to the Union military and missionaries supporting the camp residents. The federal executive branch, Army, and Navy owned the organizational skills, distribution channels, and resources needed to create a functioning camp environment.

The missionary societies had access to compassionate staff with the skills to administer camp services and set up camp schools. The contraband camps and schools were not just a part of the response but a cornerstone of the transition from enslaved people to freedom and Black communities.

The camp residents, recognizing the pivotal role of education in a free labor economy, took the initiative to set up camp schools. This initiative-taking step underscores their agency and commitment to education as a tool for empowerment, which led to the establishment of the HBCUs.

It is a testament to the transformative power of knowledge in the transition from enslaved people to free labor and from contraband camps to HBCU campuses and Black communities and towns. For example, Hampton University, an HBCU officially founded in 1868, was started near Fort Monroe, the first contraband camp.

In 1861, the American Missionary Association (AMA) responded to the camp's need for education and hired Mary Smith Peake as its first teacher. She had already secretly been teaching slaves and free Blacks in the area despite the state's legal prohibition.

She first taught for the AMA on September 17, 1861, and was said to gather her pupils under a large oak. The Emancipation Proclamation was read here under that oak tree in 1863, the first place in the Confederate States. From then on, the big tree was called the Emancipation Oak. The tree, now a symbol of the university and the city, survives as part of the designated National Historic Landmark District at Hampton University.

LeMoyne-Owen College in Memphis, Tennessee, is another example of a contraband camp to an HBCU transition. Founded in 1862 as an elementary school for freedmen, Lincoln Chapel was started at Camp Shiloh when the AMA sent Lucinda Humphrey to establish the school soon after the occupation of Memphis by Federal troops during the Civil War.

The school relocated to Memphis proper in 1863 from south of the city at Camp Shiloh. In 1866, it was destroyed during the Memphis Massacre, a white race riot that erupted following the withdrawal of federal troops. The school was rebuilt, and in 1867, it reopened with 150 students and six teachers.

However, the story did not end there. In 1870, a Pennsylvania doctor, Francis Julius, donated $20,000 to the AMA to build an elementary and secondary school for prospective teachers. LeMoyne, a notable abolitionist, traveled from his Pennsylvania home to visit the new school and donated a clock for its tower. The school opened in a newly constructed building at 284 Orleans Street in 1871, which was named LeMoyne Normal and Commercial School.

The runaway story presented in this book offers a fresh perspective on the narrative of runaway slaves, which often concludes with their return to the plantation. Here, the act of escaping serves as the foundation for an HBCU, a recurring theme among the Blacks enslaved at the onset of the Civil War.

Their action demonstrated that these Black Americans, despite the apparent hopelessness of their predicament, had plans and were waiting for the opportunity to implement them. Therefore, even today, there is no reason to dismiss the possibility that a story exists (it may be just a rumor) about a plan for the economic mobility of the most marginalized segments of the Black community.

1.3 High Cotton Freedom

The moral of Aesop's fable "The Goose That Laid the Golden Eggs" is about the dangers of greed and the importance of being content with what you have. In the story, a farmer and his wife have a goose that lays one golden egg daily. They become impatient and greedy, wanting to obtain all the golden eggs at once, so they kill the goose, only to find no more golden eggs inside. As a result, they lose their source of wealth entirely.

The key lesson of the story is that excessive greed can lead to the loss of valuable resources, and that patience and contentment are virtues. It reminds us to appreciate and wisely manage what we have rather than risk everything for immediate gain.

This lesson was lost on the Southern planters, who, like the farmer and his wife, benefited tremendously from the enslaved Black population, whose annual cotton harvest made the planters the largest exporters of cotton in the world. However, the Southern planters were not content with the wealth they gained from practicing slavery in the South.

Instead, they aimed to extend the labor of the enslaved Black population into the new territories of the United States. This ambition of the Southern planter initiated the Civil War and marked the end of slave labor, which was akin to killing the goose that laid the golden eggs.

The economic importance of the wealth generated by cotton production had not diminished after the war; however, Southern planters would no longer control it. The federal government and Northern capitalists recognized that restoring cotton production was critical to the nation's financial recovery. Cotton exports were necessary to help reduce the massive federal debt and stabilize monetary affairs to fund economic development, particularly railroads.

The Industrial Revolution created textile machinery and factories to process raw cotton, leading to clothing made from cotton. To meet the insatiable European demand for machine-made cotton products, which offered better and cheaper clothing than hand-made alternatives, cotton purchases in Europe and New England soared from 720,000 bales in 1830 to 2.85 million bales in 1850 and 5 million in 1860.

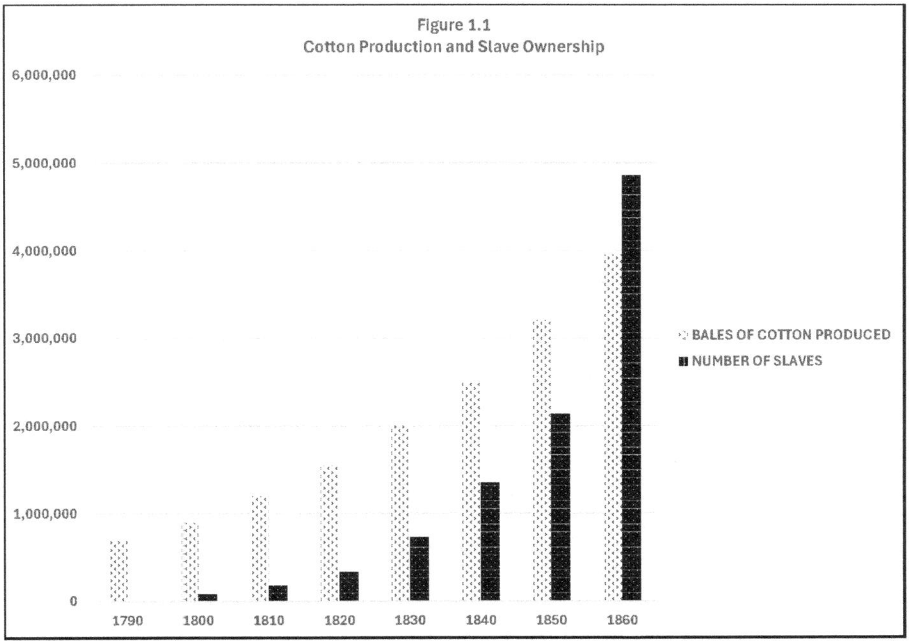

FIGURE 1.1 Cotton production and slave ownership

In response to the European demand for cotton, Southern planters invested in enslaved people, the key ingredient in cotton production, rather than in factories or land. By 1861, on the verge of the Civil War, the average planter held almost two-thirds of his wealth in the form of enslaved people and consequently lost two-thirds of their wealth, if not all of it, after the war.

Figure 1.1 illustrates the relationship between global demand for machine-made cotton clothing, slave ownership, and cotton production. After the abolition of slavery, fulfilling this demand would have been impossible without the support of a free Black labor force.

In 1860, cotton production in the United States was pivotal to the global economy, as detailed in Sven Beckert's 2014 book *Empire of Cotton: A Global History*. The South produced approximately 75 percent of the world's cotton, which was essential for the booming textile industries in Britain and other parts of Europe. This dominance in cotton production made the South a critical player in global trade and industrialization.

The vast cotton supply from the South enabled manufacturers to produce textiles on an unprecedented scale, fueling the Industrial Revolution. This, in turn, led to significant economic growth and the expansion of global capitalism. The reliance on slave labor in the South was an integral part of this financial system, as it allowed for the mass production of cotton at low costs and generated enormous profits for investors.

By 1860, cotton accounted for nearly 60 percent of American exports, totaling $200 million annually, equivalent to $3.87 billion in 2024 dollars. Cotton's central role in the national economy and its significance on the international stage led to the boast that "Cotton is King." It fostered a belief among the Southern states that secession was feasible and there was no need to fear a war with the Northern States.

The theory posited that control over cotton exports would make an independent Confederacy economically viable for New England's textile industry and—most importantly—compel Great Britain and France to support the Confederacy militarily, given that their industrial economies relied on Southern cotton.

The South is known for its long, hot summers and river deltas rich in soil, making it an ideal location for growing cotton. Additionally, the South had several ports suitable for transporting cotton to the world market. By 1860, shipments from Houston, New Orleans, Charleston, Mobile, Savannah, and a few other ports supplied cotton to the global market.

The King Cotton slogan, widely believed throughout the South, helped mobilize support for secession. By February 1861, the seven states whose economies relied on cotton plantations had all seceded and formed the Confederacy. In contrast, the other eight southern states, which had little or no cotton production, remained in the Union.

To demonstrate the alleged power of King Cotton, Southern cotton merchants spontaneously refused to ship out their cotton in early 1861. By the summer of 1861, the Union Navy blockaded every major Confederate port and shut down over 95 percent of exports.

Since the British mills had large cotton stockpiles, they suffered no immediate injury from the embargo; indeed, the value of their stockpiles soared. For Britain to have intervened would have meant war with the United States and a cut-off of food supplies.

About one-fourth of Britain's food supplies came from the United States, and American warships could destroy much of British commerce while the Royal Navy convoyed ships full of cotton. The British never believed in "King Cotton" and never intervened.

As a result, the strategy proved to be a failure for the Confederacy. King Cotton did not benefit the new nation, but the blockade prevented the urgently needed gold from cotton production from being obtained. Most importantly, this false belief led to unrealistic assumptions that the war would be won through European intervention if only the Confederacy could hold out long enough.

The biggest miscalculation of the Southern planters was their belief that the labor force producing cotton would remain loyal to their desire to secede from the Union. Instead, the enslaved laborers used the Civil War to fight for their freedom by leaving the plantation and fleeing toward the nearest Union Army line. For the enslaved Black population, this desire to expand slavery and the ensuing conflict finally provided them with the opportunity to share in the wealth generated by their cotton production.

By taking control of the Mississippi River Valley, the Union Army secured the most valuable economic asset supporting the South's war effort: cotton production. By capturing Memphis, New Orleans, and Vicksburg, the Union Army gained control of the most profitable agricultural lands in the United States, if not the world, along with the means of production—the land and labor—that remained unaffected by the war.

Initially, the Union Army's efforts to increase cotton production involved Freedmen and planters agreeing to a contract whereby Freedmen received wages for working with planters to rebuild abandoned plantations. These negotiated labor agreements between Freedmen and planters seldom succeeded because the working conditions on plantations under these agreements were too similar, if not precisely like those practiced under slavery.

In addition, the planters required more readily accessible cash to pay regular weekly wages or purchase the supplies needed to cultivate the land. This cash was not easily obtainable from Northern banks, which preferred the financial rewards of high cotton production but aimed to avoid the risks associated with agricultural production during a war.

The program that ultimately restored the Southern economy was sharecropping, a contractual agreement in which Freedmen agreed to return to the plantation and work as a family unit in exchange for a share of the harvest produced from the land. Sharecropping allowed Black families to remain together on the land, live off the land they cultivated, develop work schedules without the planter's day-to-day supervision, and require less upfront cash from the planters.

With free Black labor and sharecropping, America regained its sought-after position as the world's leading cotton producer by 1870. Sharecropping, small farmers, and plantation owners produced more cotton than they had in 1860; by 1880, they exported more cotton than in 1860.

For 134 years, from 1803 to 1937, the United States was the world's leading cotton exporter. Given this outcome and the significance of cotton production in the development of the Industrial Revolution, the formerly enslaved Black population was the goose that laid the golden egg for the South, the United States, and the world economy.

However, while sharecropping restored prewar-level cotton production, the Freedmen's preferred land program was a land confiscation and redistribution initiative authorized under Special Field Orders No. 15. This order, issued by General William Tecumseh Sherman in January 1865, approved the Union Army's confiscation of land in South Carolina, Georgia, and Florida.

These former plantations were distributed in 40 acre parcels, and provisions needed to work the land were given to 18,000 formerly enslaved Black families. These Field Orders are the source of the expression and the expectation of receiving "forty acres and a mule" among formerly enslaved families.

Establishing policies that allowed for land confiscation and redistribution in the South or anywhere in the United States was not favored by Northern business interests. Consequently, this land program ended after President Andrew Johnson (President Lincoln's successor) issued a Presidential Executive Order returning the land to the plantation owners.

After the Civil War, the Union Army's work with the runaways led to the creation of a federal agency explicitly designed to ease the transition of Black people from enslaved persons to free laborers: the Freedmen's Bureau, also known as the Bureau of Refugees, Freedmen, and Abandoned Lands. The Bureau was established in March 1865 as a temporary auxiliary of the U.S. Department of War, operating without direct funding under the direction of the Union Army.

Under the leadership of General Oliver Howard and using the funds and staff of the Union Army budget, the Bureau provided comprehensive support for the transitional needs of Freedmen. Administered by white Army officers and staffed by Black Union soldiers, the Bureau was the only federally funded entity authorized to assist the Freedmen in their transition to freedom and to provide protection from the defeated and angry Confederates.

As a federal agency authorized by Congress, the Bureau's responsibilities extended beyond the services outlined in Presidential Executive Order Proclamation 95, which provided temporary food, clothing, and shelter to establish a Black community. The Bureau employed a comprehensive approach, beginning with a family unification program to assist Freedmen in locating and reuniting with family members separated before and after the war. This role in family unification and its advocacy in local legal matters provided a reassuring presence and the necessary support for the Freedmen's transition to freedom.

The Bureau played a crucial role in developing the Black community by establishing schools that offered educational opportunities and laid the groundwork for many HBCUs. Additionally, the Bureau addressed the healthcare needs of the Black community by constructing hospitals and providing medical aid to millions of people.

The Bureau took the initiative in negotiating labor contracts between planters and the formerly enslaved, resolved labor disputes, and assisted freed individuals in securing employment. The Bureau also continued to provide millions of freed and displaced people with food, shelter, and clothing, and supported Black veterans in their transition to civilian life.

Although the Bureau was not intended to be a permanent federal agency, it also aimed to settle formerly enslaved people on land confiscated or abandoned during the war. Ultimately, the Bureau could not fully implement its programs due to a lack of funds and personnel and the political climate surrounding race and Reconstruction. What the Bureau offered was a source of protection for the establishment of the Black community, which faced constant attacks from returning Confederates.

While sharecropping did not provide land ownership, it did allow the Freedmen to establish a sustainable level of family stability that was unknown under the system of chattel slavery. It enabled them to capitalize on their agricultural knowledge of the land where they were enslaved, and purchase land.

Sharecropping revitalized agricultural production in the South while providing Freedmen families with market incentives that were absent in the Bureau's contract labor program. Sharecropping granted Freedmen the flexibility to decide how to use their family resources and the chance to provide their children with the essential education needed to thrive in a free labor economy.

Strong family units in the South were critical to the success of the Bureau's most effective program: the development of HBCUs. HBCUs enhance Freedmen's agricultural skills and enable them to earn incomes that support their families. Members of Freedmen families became students at HBCUs, and their descendants make up most of the students currently enrolled at HBCUs.

The Bureau's most transformative effort was using its Congressional authority to seize Confederate property to fund education and convert contraband camp schools into educational institutions. With the aid of missionaries, these camp schools, starting as elementary schools, eventually evolved into what we now know as HBCUs.

In the Confederate States, it was illegal to educate an enslaved person because the knowledge gained from an education was the key to dismantling the institution of slavery. It empowered the enslaved to articulate the evils of slavery and recognize themselves as men rather than enslaved people. This journey from ignorance to knowledge is a powerful testament to the liberating force of education, and the Bureau laid the groundwork for this journey.

The Bureau's education program partnered with missionaries and aid societies like the American Home Missionary Society (AHMS) and the American Missionary Association (AMA) to provide public and higher education to Freedmen families. The Bureau provided the land, and the missionaries raised the funding to finance the schools' construction, administration, and operation.

These HBCUs emphasized industrial and agricultural training, recognizing the importance of these skills in building an economically sustainable Black community. However, their top priority was providing literacy skills to the previously enslaved and training Black teachers to teach these skills.

The increase in literacy was a priority for the Freedmen and was also an essential component to obtaining the support of the Northern industrialists who funded the HBCUs. The funder's highest priority for the Bureau and the Union Army was to start a program to restore the South's cotton production to its prewar levels as soon as possible.

Therefore, combining the Bureau's most successful initiatives, sharecropping, and HBCUs, helped restore the Southern economy to pre-Civil War levels. By 1895, these efforts culminated in the Cotton States and International Exposition, a world's fair held in Atlanta, Georgia, designed to foster trade and show the region's products and facilities to the rest of the nation and the world.

The Cotton States Exposition successfully highlighted Atlanta as a business center and attracted investment to the city. After the exposition, the City of Atlanta purchased the grounds, which became Piedmont Park and the Atlanta Botanical Garden. Today, Piedmont Park is still the premier public area of Atlanta.

The fair is best known for the "Atlanta Compromise" speech by Booker T. Washington, an exemplary example of the Southern transformation that the fair attempted to showcase. Washington was formerly enslaved, an 1875 HBCU graduate of Hampton University, and the founder of Tuskegee University, an HBCU established in 1881. The speech laid the foundation for an agreement between Black and white leaders in which Black people submitted to white political rule in the South in exchange for access to education, the freedom to compete in the marketplace, and due process under the law.

The due process under the law included protecting the property rights of every citizen and fair competition in free economic markets. Black families possessed an advantage in the competition to restore cotton production to its prewar levels because their labor was responsible for creating that production level in the first place.

This direct competition between Black people and whites to increase economic production was supposed to be protected by due process of law, per the agreement outlined in the Atlanta Compromise speech. However, the success of the Black community in this intensely competitive environment spurred resentment among Southerners, who were unable to accept the change in the economic and social order after the war.

With the removal of federal troops, which protected due process under the law, white Southerners resorted to violence and the threat of violence to alter the law and marketplace competition in their favor. This resulted in Black people enduring a legal system dominated by the practice of racial discrimination that served as a legal impediment to the development of Black communities and their ability to earn the most crucial reward associated with competing in a free economy, the ability to accrue generational family wealth.

CHAPTER 2

HBCUs Forever

2.1 The Roots

The HBCUs, established after the Civil War, were part of a new economic era that the United States and the world were entering. In this era, mechanical power replaced animal-generated power as the dominant force in the economy. The end of the Civil War not only marked the conclusion of slavery in the United States but also represented a victory for mechanical power, positioning the United States to lead the world into this new era.

The merger of mechanical power with human labor promised to elevate labor productivity beyond any level achieved using animal-generated power and human labor. This new merger requires providing the workforce with the education and training to develop a highly skilled workforce capable of constructing and operating machinery driven by mechanical power.

Therefore, every American institution of higher education, including the newly established HBCUs, was on a mission to create the highly skilled workforce demanded by Northern industrialists after the end of the Civil War. Mastering mechanical power increases labor and capital productivity, producing more goods and services in the same amount of time with the same number of resources. The transformation would elevate the United States into the world's leading industrial power.

With this highly skilled workforce, Northern industrialists could concentrate on developing a national market to capitalize on their enhanced capacity to produce goods and services. They aimed to connect the national market with a railroad system linking the Atlantic Ocean to the Pacific Ocean and every major city and town in between.

After the Civil War, Northern industrialists invested their financial resources in building this national market and railroad network, which captured the economic markets of the United States and the world. Completing the national market, railroad network, and industrial production of goods and services proved to be a tremendous financial success, leading the United States into a period of unprecedented prosperity—the Gilded Age.

Rapid industrialization, economic growth, technological advancements, and world market domination characterized the Gilded Age. The term referred to the unprecedented wealth of Northern industrialists who invested in the national market and railroad network.

This period in U.S. history lasted from the late 1870s to the early 1900s, and the wealth generated during the Gilded Age provided the resources necessary to restore the economy of the Southern states and establish HBCUs as part of that effort.

The HBCUs created during this period were privately financed by Northern abolitionists, who were now also wealthy industrialists and philanthropists. They continued the missionaries' efforts to establish schools specifically designed to meet the educational needs of the previously enslaved.

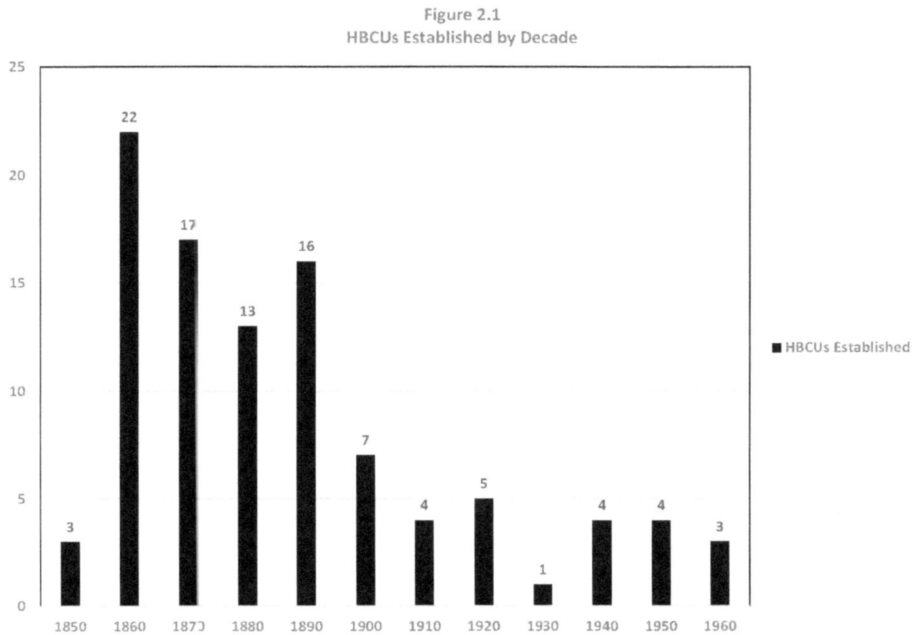

FIGURE 2.1 HBCUs founded by decade

Figure 2.1 illustrates the success of the collaboration between Northern industrialist philanthropy, the missionaries, and the Freedmen's Bureau in establishing HBCUs during the South's reconstruction. The data indicate that an average of three HBCUs were established in each of the states of the defeated Confederacy during the twenty years following the war.

Some of the first privately funded institutions included Clark Atlanta University (1865), Shaw University (1865), Fisk University (1866), Howard University (1867), Morehouse College (1867), Hampton University (1868), and Dillard University (1868).

These institutions and most HBCUs are named after major financial contributors who provided the crucial funding or administrative support needed to start the institution. HBCUs were founded, funded, and operated by white abolitionists and philanthropists and would not exist today without their financial assistance.

For example, Spelman College, one of the most academically successful and financially endowed HBCUs today, was founded by one of the best-known philanthropists of the Gilded Age. Laura Spelman Rockefeller, whose family was a longtime activist in the abolitionist movement, was also the wife of John D. Rockefeller, the founder of Standard Oil.

HBCUs were built to provide elementary and secondary education to children and illiterate adults, and eventually evolved into higher education institutions. They were established to provide a comprehensive liberal arts education, preparing students for careers as teachers and ministers equipped with the skills, courage, and temperament to duplicate the missionaries' work in public school systems throughout the Southern states.

These teachers, ministers, and missionaries were required to transform the illiterate, previously enslaved Black laborers into the skilled workers needed to produce the goods and services for the national marketplace envisioned by the industrialists. In addition, the knowledge provided by the HBCU graduate would generate families and communities of consumers for the national market.

But, before they could become institutions of higher learning, the future students of the HBCUs had to learn the basic principles of education because the enslaved population lived under anti-literacy laws. The origins of anti-literacy laws date back to the 1700s and were rooted in the belief that Black literacy posed a threat to the institution of slavery.

Violating anti-literacy laws carried severe penalties for teaching enslaved people to read or write, including fines, imprisonment, and even physical punishment. The exact penalties vary by state and could be harsh, reflecting the severe resistance to the idea of educating enslaved individuals.

Anti-literacy laws were regulations enacted primarily in the Southern United States between the eighteenth and nineteenth centuries. They were designed to prohibit enslaved and, in some cases, free Black Americans from learning to read or write.

Whites feared that literate enslaved people could forge documents needed to prove their freedom upon escape or incite others to escape. This fear was reinforced after Nat Turner, an enslaved preacher, led his congregation in rebellion in 1831. After that, anti-literacy laws became more entrenched and widespread throughout the South.

Anti-literacy laws severely limited educational opportunities for Black people in the United States, contributing to long-term disparities in literacy, education, and the skills required to earn income in an industrialized economy. Therefore, the establishment of HBCUs was needed to reverse the effect of anti-literacy laws and equip previously enslaved labor with the educational skills necessary to participate in an industrialized economy—the ability to read, write, and perform basic arithmetic, the three Rs.

The origins of the HBCUs started in the contraband camps maintained by the Union Army, where missionary groups set up camp schools to teach camp residents the basics of education, beginning at the elementary level. By the end of the Civil War, over one hundred contraband camps and camp schools were designed to instruct children and adults in the three Rs.

Consequently, 90 percent of the HBCUs are in the states of the old Confederacy, and over one hundred of the original HBCUs are still in operation today. These schools were administered by white missionaries or church groups and built with funding provided by Northern industrial philanthropists and evolved into HBCUs to offer higher education to Black students who were excluded from attending white institutions.

HBCUs evolved into hubs of empowerment and advocacy, cultivating a sense of community and resilience among Black students. These institutions fostered African Americans' cultural and intellectual development and promoted literacy and education as indispensable tools for social change.

HBCUs educated the Black leaders who formed communities, churches, secondary schools, and markets to serve this previously enslaved population. The establishment of HBCUs represented a critical advancement in dismantling the legacy of slavery and anti-literacy laws and facilitating the transformation of Blacks in America.

The Freedmen's Bureau, led by Union Army white officers and staffed by Black soldiers, provided support and protection to the governors appointed to administer the Reconstruction of the South, which started in 1865 and ended in 1876. This support and protection were extended to the HBCUs, allowing this educational effort to take root.

This structure of support and protection also allowed Northern Black people, former white Union soldiers, teachers, professionals, and entrepreneurs to immigrate in large numbers from the North into the South to pursue economic opportunities after the war. These immigrants played an essential role in establishing HBCUs and served as leaders of these institutions during the Reconstruction period.

The original HBCUs used a teaching curriculum method called "normal" schools, which refers to these institutions' goal of instilling and reinforcing norms within students. "Norms" included historical behavioral standards of the time and norms that reinforced targeted societal values, ideologies, and dominant narratives in the curriculum.

This system was used to develop the higher education systems of the Northern states before the Civil War, transforming the Northern labor force and the United States labor force into an industrial world power. The educators of the North who immigrated to the South to staff the HBCUs transferred this teaching technique to the South, which enhanced the effectiveness of HBCUs in developing an educational network for the Black community.

The normal school model served as an efficient and effective means for the HBCUs' educational network to start producing the teachers and preachers needed to spread the norms required to develop stable families and communities with a strong emphasis on education and human morality. The norms of the HBCUs would evolve as their leadership was transferred from the original white administrators to the graduates of the HBCUs, and the word " normal" was dropped from the name of these institutions.

Under the leadership of HBCU graduates, the HBCU norms would evolve to include the elements of the African heritage of the previously enslaved and the need to address the practice of racial discrimination that accommodated their enslavement. However, the leadership of these institutions would remain tied to their original funding sources, which would eventually conflict with the students' desire to participate in the Civil Rights Movement.

2.2 The Fruits

Any financial or organizational efforts by Northern industrial philanthropists and missionaries to establish HBCUs for the education of previously enslaved Black people in the South would have been wasted if not accompanied by federal political actions that rewarded the Black population's contribution to the North's Civil War victory. The United States Congress passed the Reconstruction Act of 1867 and three amendments to the Constitution: the 13th Amendment, which abolished slavery; the 14th Amendment, which provided citizenship rights and equal protection under the law; and the 15th Amendment, which provided voting rights.

These federal actions ensured the Black population and the newly established HBCUs would be provided with some degree of protection from former Confederate soldiers returning to the South after the war. In addition, these federal actions made it possible for the transformation of the enslaved to start in the South, despite the ambiguity that existed regarding their transformation before the war.

The Reconstruction Act of 1867 temporarily divided the South into five military districts. It mandated that Southern states ratify the 14th Amendment, which expanded the definition of citizenship to grant "equal protection" of the Constitution to formerly enslaved people before they could rejoin the Union, and the 15th Amendment, which guaranteed that a citizen's right to vote would not be denied "on account of race, color, or previous condition of servitude."

By 1870, all the former Confederate states had been admitted to the Union, and the state constitutions approved by the Radical Republicans during Reconstruction were the most progressive in the region's history. The participation of Black people in Southern public life after 1867 would be the most radical development of Reconstruction and a large-scale experiment in interracial democracy.

These laws not only represented changes for Southern state governments but also impacted all state governments. Prior to the ratification of these amendments to the Constitution, not every state had granted voting rights or citizenship to its Black population. While the Reconstruction Act primarily targeted the South, the Reconstruction Amendments transformed the United States' democracy by uniformly defining the terms of citizenship and voting rights for the nation.

The Reconstruction Act and the Reconstruction Amendments changed and improved the laws governing the United States' democracy. However, changing the law did not change the practice of racial discrimination, which was embedded in the American way of life at its inception.

The state constitutions that the Radical Republicans developed and approved for the former Confederate states were more democratically advanced than any of their states in the Union. Consequently, the Radical Republican version of Reconstruction, which President Andrew Johnson vetoed, would eventually be challenged.

Meanwhile, in the South, Black males registered to vote and, with voter turnout exceeding 90 percent, won the election for the Republican Party and the control of every former Confederate state government. These first-time Republican victories in the South created biracial leadership in Southern state governments and the U.S. Congress during this period.

These political victories resulted in the most enduring of the Reconstruction achievements: the South's first state-funded public school systems. Between 1868 and 1870, the eleven states of the Confederacy incorporated provisions requiring public education into their constitutions: Alabama, Arkansas, Florida, Georgia, Louisiana, Mississippi, North and South Carolina in 1868, Texas and Virginia in 1869, and Tennessee in 1870.

The public schools established by the biracial leadership of the Southern states fueled the industrialization of the South by transforming slave labor into free labor and providing students for the HBCUs. These public education systems were funded by property taxes levied on property owners but also benefited from the Freedmen Bureau's initiative to establish schools, which helped develop and build public schools, some of which eventually evolved into HBCUs.

The schools established by the Freedmen's Bureau that did not become institutions of higher learning continued to operate as elementary and secondary schools and became part of the state-funded public school system. The public schools that provided elementary and secondary education supplied the HBCUs with students who would return to the Black community as teachers, preachers, and entrepreneurs.

Rebuilding the South's economy to its prewar level required massive amounts of materials produced in Northern plants. It demonstrated the strategy's effectiveness in utilizing the national market and railroad network of Northern industrialists. Supplying the necessary goods and services to rebuild the South presented a tremendous economic opportunity to illustrate the profitability of the new industrial era.

Another essential component of rebuilding the South was transforming the slave labor force that had driven prewar economic production into a free labor force capable of matching or exceeding prewar production levels during the postwar industrial era. To achieve this goal, Northern investments in the South's reconstruction also included funding to establish HBCUs.

By the end of Reconstruction, immigrants from the Northern states comprised the administrative staff and faculty of the HBCUs, initiated businesses to rebuild Southern cities, made investments to finance Southern planters, and were elected to government positions overseeing the Southern states. These unique circumstances enabled HBCUs to establish the foundations of an educational network that continues today in the heart of the old Confederacy.

Once established, HBCUs continued to grow after Reconstruction, when the Union Army's protection left the South in 1876 and into the twentieth century due to changes in the Morrill Land-Grant Acts. The Morrill Act, which passed on July 2, 1862, provided states with federal land grants to fund higher education institutions and supply the training necessary to improve the productivity of the Northern labor force. The act granted the states large tracts of federal land and permitted them to sell a portion of the land to raise funds for building and operating higher education institutions.

Sponsored by Senator Justin Smith Morrill of Vermont, the Act allocated 30,000 acres of public land to each state for each member of Congress. The proceeds from the sale of this land were designated to fund the establishment of colleges emphasizing agriculture and the mechanical arts.

This legislation significantly broadened access to higher education, particularly for farmers and working-class individuals. By promoting education in agriculture and mechanical disciplines, the Morrill Act facilitated the economic development of the United States, especially in rural areas. Consequently, land-grant universities emerged as vital centers for research and innovation, advancing fields such as agriculture and engineering.

The Morrill Act of 1862 did not significantly impact the state's higher education system until after the Civil War ended in 1865, when resources and men were available to participate. At this time, the benefits of the Acts were not extended to Black students due to the segregation prevalent in many land-grant institutions.

However, the Second Morrill Act of 1890 sought to remedy this inequity by mandating the establishment of separate land-grant institutions for Black students if they were denied admission to existing institutions funded by the Morrill Act. This led to the creation of approximately fifty HBCUs in the Southern states, and a second surge of HBCUs was established at the beginning of the twentieth century.

By the time the Second Morrill Act passed, the HBCU educational network had acquired twenty-five years of experience starting in 1865. Therefore, the network was adequately prepared to develop universities designed to educate the Black population.

This federal support was instrumental in sustaining and expanding HBCUs, further enhancing their role in providing educational access and promoting literacy. This legislative change established state-funded HBCUs, which received state and federal funds to improve their teaching, research capabilities, and extension services.

The 1890 Morrill Act increased educational opportunities for Black students, solidifying the role of HBCUs as land-grant institutions. The infusion of state and federal funding significantly bolstered HBCUs' infrastructure, academic programs, and research potential.

These institutions have played an essential role in educating generations of Black leaders and professionals, contributing to Black communities' social and economic advancement. The Morrill Acts laid a foundational framework for a more inclusive and accessible higher education system in the United States, yielding enduring impacts on American society and HBCUs. So, by the time the 1960s Great Society program designation was created, there were approximately 105 HBCUs, half private and half publicly funded.

The HBCU educational network was patterned after the same public and higher education institutions established in the Northern states, which received funding from the Morrill Land Grant Acts before the war. HBCUs were established throughout the South with support from the Freedmen's Bureau, missionaries, aid societies, philanthropists, and the Morrill Land-Grant Acts of 1862 and 1890.

Under the protection of the Freedman Bureau, these communities were centered around schools and churches and revived Southern agricultural production to levels that exceeded prewar production. These HBCU students provided elementary and secondary education to the children of the Black communities that grew out of the contraband camps, which provided the first efforts toward establishing free Black communities in the South.

This educational network distributed the knowledge required to transform an enslaved population of 4 million into a Black community of 47 million, making up about 14 percent of the total U.S. population as of 2023. These HBCU-derived communities are estimated to contribute over $1.4 trillion to the U.S. GDP annually.

Based on data from the U.S. Census Bureau, the largest concentration of Black people, at 58 percent, still resides in the eleven states of the old Confederacy, the District of Columbia, and five border states: Delaware, Kentucky, Maryland, Missouri, and West Virginia. The second-highest concentration of Black people, at 31 percent, resides in the urban areas of the eight Great Migration destination states: California, Illinois, Indiana, Michigan, Missouri, New York, Ohio, and Pennsylvania. These states contain large metropolitan areas, including Los Angeles, Chicago, Indianapolis, Detroit, St. Louis, New York, Cleveland, and Philadelphia, which attracted the HBCU-trained workforce seeking economic opportunities not available in the South due to the legal practice of racial discrimination.

2.3 The Seeds

The Reconstruction period brought several significant benefits to the Black population in the South, including the abolition of slavery, the granting of citizenship, and the provision of voting rights. This allowed Black men to vote, hold public office, and establish communities that fostered a stable family structure for the previously enslaved Black population.

The formerly enslaved people took advantage of the HBCU educational network that provided schools, training, skills, and knowledge needed to transform the Black population. Freedmen could seek employment, acquire land, and start businesses, which helped improve their economic status.

The Civil Rights Act of 1866 and other legislation provided legal protection against discrimination and violence. The Freedmen's Bureau provided essential services, including food, housing, and medical care, to help newly freed individuals transition to freedom.

These benefits were crucial in helping the Black population of the South build lives and communities after the Civil War. However, the gains made during Reconstruction faced significant opposition and were often eroded in the following years.

The economic and political advances of the Black community brought about by the Reconstruction Act of 1867 were met with resentment by a growing number of Southern whites who chose to resort to violence instead of accepting the fact that the Black community could meet the challenges of freedom. Southern Democrats and former Confederates targeted local Republican leaders—both white and Black—who challenged white authority at the voting booth and in the marketplace.

Although federal legislation passed during President Ulysses S. Grant's administration in 1871 aimed to protect the Black vote, property ownership, and political rights, Southern whites gradually regained control over the South in the early 1870s as support for Reconstruction diminished among Northerners. Racism remained a powerful force in both the South and the North, and Republicans became more conservative and less committed to egalitarian ideals as the decade progressed.

In 1874, an economic depression plunged much of the South into poverty, leading to the return of the Democratic Party's control of the House of Representatives for the first time since the Civil War. In 1875, Democrats, representing the landed aristocracy of Mississippi, used a strategy known as the Mississippi Plan to regain political control of the state government through violence and intimidation.

First, the plan aimed at persuading and coercing white Republicans to abandon Black Republicans involved utilizing social, political, and economic pressure, threats of ostracism, and financial repercussions. The second part of the plan employed paramilitary groups and rifle clubs to intimidate Black voters and suppress their participation in Republican rallies by provoking violence, which led to riots and massacres where armed Democrats attacked Black Republicans. These actions effectively suppressed Black voting and enabled Democrats to regain control of the Mississippi state government.

President Grant's decision not to send federal troops after Democrats used violence to seize control of Mississippi in 1875 signaled the end of federal support for Reconstruction-era state governments in the South. By 1876, only Florida, Louisiana, and South Carolina remained under Republican control, as every Southern state adopted its version of the Mississippi Plan.

In the contentious presidential election of that year, Republican candidate Rutherford B. Hayes reached a compromise with Democrats in Congress. In exchange for certifying his election, he acknowledged Democratic control over the entire South. The Compromise of 1876 effectively marked the end of Reconstruction as a distinct period.

However, the struggle to address the changes brought about by the abolition of slavery would continue in the South and beyond long after this time. A century later, the legacy of the Reconstruction era's failure resurfaced during the Civil Rights Movement of the 1960s, as Black people fought for the political, economic, and social equality they had gained during the Reconstruction period.

The social, economic, and political transformations of the Black community during the Reconstruction of the Southern United States were interrupted from 1900 to 1950 by the legal use of racial discrimination.

This legal practice of racial discrimination was economically devastating for African Americans in the South, participating in the sharecropping system that revived cotton production but placed them in a perpetuated cycle of debt and poverty.

This system denied Black farmers any chance of competing fairly against Southern planters who controlled the outcome of any transactional dispute. The Black farmers were provided with no means to dispute the ownership of land, the distribution of the cotton harvest, or the price of the cotton that was not subject to racial discrimination.

In pursuit of improved economic opportunities and to escape the oppressive realities of legal racial discrimination, many HBCU alumni and Black households relocated to urban centers in the North, Midwest, and West. This migration had profound implications for the demographics and social dynamics of the Southern states.

During this period, HBCUs provided a place of refuge by helping the Southern Black communities establish robust social networks, churches, and institutions that provided essential support and cultivated a strong sense of identity and resilience despite these adversities. These educational institutions serving Black students were significantly underfunded and faced considerable disparities when compared to their white counterparts. Nevertheless, education remained a priority, leading to the emergence of many Black leaders from these communities.

Meanwhile, outside of the South, HBCU alumni (W.E.B. Du Bois and Ida B. Wells) were instrumental in creating organizations such as the National Association for the Advancement of Colored People (NAACP), which played a vital role in advocating for civil rights and actively challenging segregation and discrimination. Many HBCU alumni remained in the South as administrators, faculty, and staff of HBCUs and public schools established for the Black population as part of the HBCU educational network. However, many other graduates of these institutions started to leave the South for the North in large numbers.

The Great Migration refers to the movement of over six million Black Americans from the rural South to urban centers in the North, Midwest, and West between 1916 and 1970. This relocation was primarily motivated by unsatisfactory economic conditions and stringent segregationist laws that legalized the practice of racial discrimination in the South.

Migration to urban areas resulted in the expansion of Black neighborhoods and the emergence of a vibrant urban culture led by HBCU alumni. By the end of 1919, it is estimated that one million Black individuals had left the South to escape the violence that accompanied the racial inequality and segregationist policies, and to pursue economic opportunities that were denied by racial discrimination, which became institutionalized in the South.

Many Black Americans sought opportunities in Northern cities due to the increased demand for industrial labor during World War I. Throughout the Great Migration, Black individuals established a significant presence in public life, actively confronting racial discrimination and addressing economic, political, and social challenges.

Between 1910 and 1920, the Black population in major Northern cities experienced significant growth, evidenced by increases such as 66 percent in New York City, 148 percent in Chicago, 500 percent in Philadelphia, and 611 percent in Detroit. Many newcomers secured employment in factories, slaughterhouses, and foundries, and female migrants encountered more significant challenges in finding employment, leading to heightened competition for domestic labor positions.

In addition to the competition for jobs, the influx of residents has increased demand for living space in densely populated urban areas. Although segregation was not formally legislated in the North, racism and prejudice have remained prevalent.

Following the U.S. Supreme Court's 1917 ruling that deemed racially based housing ordinances unconstitutional, some neighborhoods implemented covenants mandating that white property owners could not sell to Black individuals; these covenants persisted until being invalidated by the Court in 1948.

Rising rents in segregated neighborhoods exacerbated tensions between Black and white residents nationwide. The summer of 1919 marked the beginning of the most intense period of interracial conflict in U.S. history up to that point, characterized by a troubling wave of race riots.

Led by HBCU alumni, many Black residents established self-sufficient communities within larger cities, contributing to the emergence of a distinct urban Black culture. A prominent example of this phenomenon is Harlem in New York City, which transitioned from an all-white neighborhood to one populated by approximately 200,000 Black residents by the 1920s.

The Black experience during the Great Migration became a central theme of the artistic movement known initially as the New Negro Movement and, subsequently, as the Harlem Renaissance, which profoundly influenced the cultural landscape of the era. HBCU alumni were notable artists who participated in the New Negro Movement or the Harlem Renaissance.

Langston Hughes was an influential poet, novelist, and playwright who attended Lincoln University. Zora Neale Hurston is a renowned writer and anthropologist who attended Howard University. Aaron Douglas, a prominent painter and a central figure in the Harlem Renaissance, taught at Fisk University. Duke Ellington was a legendary jazz musician closely associated with Howard University. Romare Bearden and Jacob Lawrence attended Howard University and studied under the renowned artist and educator Alain Locke, who significantly influenced their work and the Harlem Renaissance movement.

Furthermore, the Great Migration initiated a new phase of political activism among Black Americans, which gained national attention after the 1960 presidential elections. After experiencing disenfranchisement in the South, they discovered opportunities for participating in public life in Northern and Western cities.

For example, Asa Philip Randolph was an American labor unionist and civil rights activist, born in 1889 and raised in Florida. He was educated at Bethune-Cookman University, an HBCU in Jacksonville, Florida. Barred by discrimination from all but manual jobs in the South, Randolph moved to New York City in 1911, where he worked odd jobs and took social sciences courses at City College.

There, he became convinced that overcoming racism required collective action and was drawn to socialism and workers' rights. He ran unsuccessfully for state office on the socialist ticket in the early 1920s but achieved tremendous success organizing for the rights of African American workers.

In 1925, he organized and led the Brotherhood of Sleeping Car Porters, the first successful African American-led labor union. His ongoing efforts, supported by fellow labor rights activists, contributed to President Franklin D. Roosevelt issuing Executive Order 8802 in 1941, which banned discrimination in the defense industries during World War II.

The group then successfully maintained pressure until President Harry S. Truman issued Executive Orders 9980 and 9981 in 1948, promoting fair employment and anti-discrimination policies in federal government hiring and ending racial segregation in the armed services.

The Great Migration created enhanced economic opportunities for HBCU graduates in the North and other regions, enabling them to secure better-paying jobs and contribute to the economic development of their communities. Furthermore, increased enrollment and the accomplishments of HBCU graduates propelled the growth of these institutions, allowing for the expansion of their programs, facilities, and overall influence.

As Black families relocated from the South to urban areas in the North, Midwest, and West, a corresponding shift in the demographics of students attending HBCUs was observed. Many migrating families continued to value the educational offerings of HBCUs and used their higher incomes to educate their children at HBCUs, thereby increasing enrollment from diverse geographic regions.

The influx of students from various areas enriched the student body at HBCUs, improving the quality of education and fostering a broader exchange of ideas. The Great Migration facilitated a cultural exchange that significantly influenced the curricula and campus life at HBCUs.

Students introduced various artistic practices, traditions, and perspectives, collectively shaping the cultural atmosphere of these institutions. Additionally, upon returning from WWII, Black soldiers found that the GI Bill offered more uniformly guaranteed, equitable postwar benefits when used at HBCUs.

By the 1970s, a significant demographic transformation had taken place, signaling the end of the Great Migration. In 1900, nine out of ten Black Americans lived in the South, with three out of four residing on farms. By 1970, only half of the nation's Black population was still in the South, and just 20 percent occupied rural areas. This migration helped create a network of educated Black Americans who played a vital role in advocating for social and political reform.

This effort contributed to developing a vibrant Black urban culture that influenced HBCUs in subsequent decades. The Great Migration significantly impacted HBCUs as migration among Black Americans slowed during the 1930s due to the onset of the Great Depression, but resumed with World War II, creating a heightened demand for wartime production.

Although Black Americans faced discrimination in the labor market, they also encountered new opportunities in industrial employment, particularly during and after World War II. These factors greatly influenced the development of the Black American community in the South during the first half of the twentieth century, planting the seeds for the Civil Rights Movement that would gain momentum in the 1950s and 1960s.

CHAPTER 3

One Hundred Years

3.1 Soul Power

One hundred and twenty-eight years before the United States created the HBCU designation to address the educational needs of Black American youth, the Black community of Philadelphia established the first HBCU to provide Black youth with primary education and training to become tradespeople, teachers, or merchants. The first HBCUs that were established before the start of the Civil War and are still in operation today include Cheyney University (1837), Lincoln University (1851), the University of the District of Columbia (1851), and Wilberforce University (1856).

These institutions are a testament to the resilience of the Black community in their struggle to acquire the knowledge required to survive by any means necessary. The establishment of these schools signified active resistance against racial discrimination and the institution of slavery by free Blacks in the United States before the beginning of the Civil War.

Driven by what appears to be an intangible spiritual connection, these people of African descent systematically gathered into groups to help one another. These schools exemplify this unwavering determination of the free Black community to educate its youth and provide training to compete and thrive in the free marketplace, despite lacking essential financial resources.

The limitations of financial support available from church missionaries, community organizations, and philanthropists who participated in these early attempts to establish HBCUs were especially emphasized when compared to the funding accessible for the education of colonial youth of European descent.

By 1837, when the first HBCU was established, over 50 higher education institutions had been founded in the United States, and 16 of the 26 states had at least one within their borders. From their inception, colleges in the United States profoundly and positively impacted American society's economic growth. However, as a general practice, these colleges excluded Black American students and communities from the educational benefits they provided.

The South's attack on Fort Sumter on April 12, 1861, led to a surge in abolitionist, missionary, and Northern support for the cause of the enslaved, which ultimately ensured the North's victory. The conviction that God granted every person the right to freedom gave the North the moral high ground. The Battle Hymn of the Republic, written in 1861, became a rallying cry for the Union during the Civil War. Its stirring lyrics and martial melody inspired both soldiers and civilians, reinforcing the moral cause of the war, especially the fight against slavery.

The signing of the Emancipation Proclamation in 1863 finally provided the financial support and momentum necessary for establishing enough HBCUs to effectively address the challenge of educating the previously enslaved community. The proclamation was based on the Union Army's unofficial response to Black families' efforts to self-emancipate by escaping to the nearest Union Army line; it officially authorized the Union Army to financially support and safeguard the formation of Black families and communities.

The proclamation provided freedom to Black families with the courage to seek protection behind the nearest Union lines, and it gave the Union Army permission to establish contraband camps and camp schools. Initially staffed and administered by missionaries, the camp schools would evolve into public schools and eventually become HBCUs, whose graduates would produce teachers for the public education system and become future leaders of the Black community.

After the Civil War, the Freedmen's Bureau was created as a temporary auxiliary of the U.S. Army to continue the Union Army's work of supporting the development of Black families and communities. Using congressional authority to acquire land in the South for educational purposes, the Bureau provided the site for the HBCU and protected the growth of the surrounding Black communities. The Northern missionary groups offered the funding to build and administer the HBCU, marking a significant milestone in empowering the Black population.

The Bureau aimed to enforce and protect the changes implemented during Reconstruction after the war, which included necessary adjustments to integrate the self-emancipated Black population into the fabric of the reformed Southern society. These adjustments involved safeguarding the Freedmen's right to vote, which resulted in the election of Black individuals to government leadership roles and establishing the first biracial governments in the Southern states.

The rise of biracial government leadership in former Confederate states led to establishing a public school education system, a significant development that had not existed before the war. Upon returning to the Union, the new Southern state leadership recognized that public education served as a catalyst for the recovery process and the transition to an economy dominated by free rather than slave labor. It would benefit all Southerners and instill a sense of optimism and hope among them.

The economic benefits of participating in free labor markets, which required an educated labor force, significantly increased the demand for teachers and higher education institutions in the South. As Southern state governments recognized the advantages of an educated labor force, free labor not only helped restore the South's economy to its prewar level but also instilled a sense of reassurance and confidence in the future of HBCUs.

Ending the practice of chattel slavery and creating HBCUs were the most significant accomplishments of the Civil War and proved to have the most direct economic benefit on the Black population. The Union Army and the Freedmen's Bureau provided the protection and time needed for these Reconstruction-era accomplishments to take hold and have the desired effect.

Nevertheless, the growth of HBCUs spurred controversy among prominent Black educators in the late nineteenth and early twentieth centuries. The main controversy involved whether the Black community is better served by HBCUs that pursue vocational training or a more classically "intellectual" education.

Educated at Hampton University, Booker T. Washington advocated for vocational training and agricultural and industrial education. Educated at Fisk University and Harvard University, trained sociologist W. E. B. Du Bois supported an intellectual approach. Washington envisioned a separate but equal social structure to enable Black people to build independent communities capable of competing in a free marketplace. Conversely, Du Bois envisioned cultivating a "talented tenth" of well-educated Black community leaders to be immediately admitted into the social structure without restrictions.

Both positions in this debate recognize the lack of freedom and economic independence caused by the legal practice of racial discrimination both within and outside the South. Both sides of the controversy represent a compromise by acknowledging how racial discrimination practices in the United States prevent the Black population from participating freely in the nation's society or competing in the market economy.

Washington advocated a policy that allowed racial discrimination by permitting the Black population to participate equally in the marketplace while maintaining separate involvement in other areas. Similarly, Du Bois promoted a policy that accepted racial discrimination by designating 10 percent of the Black population as eligible for immediate equal participation in all aspects of society. In comparison, the remaining 90 percent continued to prepare for eventual equal participation.

These accommodations shaped the leadership of most HBCUs, which remained cautious about their actions to support the development of the Black community residing beyond their walls. Their efforts centered on preparing students within their walls to face the challenges awaiting them once they left the HBCU's protection.

Some critics noted that many HBCUs were founded by whites who held negative preconceptions about the capabilities of Black people and practiced racial discrimination. Consequently, the quality of education provided at these HBCUs did not adequately prepare their students to compete successfully in a free society or the free market.

Despite the debates, by establishing a publicly financed public school education system, the Reconstruction-era biracial Southern governments created a process that necessitated the establishment of HBCUs to produce teachers and a funding mechanism to facilitate this. The states funded the salaries of schools and teachers by taxing property owners. Parents of public school graduates pay tuition to HBCUs so their children can become teachers, preachers, medical professionals, and more. After graduating from HBCUs, they receive salaries for teaching public school students from the state, providing medical services, and offering the spiritual guidance needed to support the community.

The Washington versus Du Bois debate is one of those discussions that can only be settled after decades of collecting data from the experiment's outcomes. Analyzing the data gathered over the last century on the impact of the HBCU educational network provides evidence to support the success of both arguments while reaching the same conclusion.

The development of HBCUs in the South was essential to the survival of the Black population as the Southern states' governments took steps to legalize the practice of racial discrimination. According to Du Bois, if it were not for HBCUs, "the Negro would for all intents and purposes, have been driven back to slavery." Not only are HBCUs responsible for forming the Black middle class in America, but they have produced the majority of Black judges, doctors, teachers, social workers, military officers, and civil rights leaders.

After the Civil War and the emancipation of enslaved people, there was a significant need for educational institutions to serve Black Americans. The Reconstruction era established many HBCUs to provide higher education opportunities. The Southern state governments' legalization of racial segregation after Reconstruction severely limited educational opportunities for Black Americans, which were limited before the Civil War. HBCUs were founded to counteract these restrictions and provide a space for Black Americans to pursue higher education.

Many HBCUs received funding and support from philanthropic organizations and religious groups committed to improving education for African Americans. Acts like the Morrill Land-Grant Acts provided federal support for establishing colleges, including HBCUs. This support was crucial in establishing and sustaining these institutions. Black communities played a vital role in advocating for and supporting the establishment of HBCUs. These institutions became centers for community development and empowerment.

However, there was a more significant debate between the Northern and Southern states about which freedoms and rights would be permanently granted to Black people after the Civil War. The Reconstruction Amendments to the Constitution (13th, 14th, and 15th Amendments) provided rights at the federal level but no provisions or directions on how to enforce these rights at the state or local level of government after Reconstruction, which provided ten regiments of Black Union soldiers as a means of protection and enforcement.

The debate centered around the implementation plan for protecting and enforcing the Reconstruction Act of 1867, which some argued may have been too radical for a permanent solution. Still, a reasonable compromise is not the complete reversal of the rights earned by the previously enslaved after the Civil War, which became the goal of the Southern state governments after the withdrawal of federal troops in 1876.

Persuading the federal government to protect and enforce the rights gained by the Black community for participating in the Civil War became the sole responsibility of the HBCUs after the Republican Party's loss of political control of the South.

However, the success of the HBCU-trained Black labor force often elicited a violent response from segments of the white population. Many whites could not successfully compete against this recently educated addition to the private and public sectors of the free marketplace.

White acts of violence against the economic aspirations of the developing Black community often overshadow the success and cooperation achieved during this period. The following list briefly describes some of the worst riots of white-against-Black violence provoked by the economic advancements of the Black community.

Wilmington Insurrection (1898): A violent overthrow of the elected biracial government in Wilmington, North Carolina, by white supremacists, resulting in the deaths of many Black residents and the destruction of Black-owned businesses and homes.

Atlanta Race Riot (1906): A series of violent attacks by white mobs against Black residents in Atlanta, Georgia, was caused by competition for jobs, housing, political power, and the influence of inflammatory political rhetoric during a heated gubernatorial campaign.

Springfield Race Riot (1908): A mob consisting of about 5,000 white Americans and European immigrants attacked Black neighborhoods, murdering Black citizens and destroying Black businesses and homes. The violence was symptomatic of the racial tensions and fears of racial equality that existed in both the North and South at the time.

East St. Louis Riot (1917): A brutal attack by white mobs on Black residents in East St. Louis, Illinois; the immediate cause was the employment of Black American workers in factories holding government contracts, which led to resentment among white workers and to many deaths and widespread destruction.

Chicago Race Riot (1919): Part of the "Red Summer" of 1919, this riot involved violent clashes between white and Black residents in Chicago, Illinois, as returning white soldiers from World War I found their jobs taken by Black Americans and immigrants, leading to heightened racial tensions, resulting in numerous deaths and injuries.

Tulsa Race Massacre (1921): One of the most devastating incidents, where white mobs attacked the prosperous Black community of Greenwood (known as Black Wall Street) in Tulsa, Oklahoma, leading to the deaths of hundreds of Black residents and the destruction of the entire neighborhood.

However, these acts of violence were not sufficient deterrents to stop the economic advancement of the Black community. The following is a list of Black millionaires from the early 1900s who rose above the violence perpetrated by whites. Their success stories transformed Black enslaved labor into a free labor force that succeeded.

William Alexander Leidesdorff, often regarded as America's first Black millionaire, amassed wealth in California through commerce and real estate. Mary Ellen Pleasant also acquired her wealth from California through the Gold Rush and used it to support abolitionist causes.

Robert Reed Church, the son of a riverboat captain from Memphis, Tennessee, used his earnings to become the largest landowner in Tennessee. After her husband's death, Hannah Elias built a real estate empire in Harlem. Annie Turnbo Malone developed the first national brand of hair care products, followed by Madam C. J.

Walker, who built a successful business empire with her hair care products and became the first Black woman millionaire.

The Southern Democratic Party (SDP) and the HBCUs were now engaged in a war over how the federal government should implement the rights gained by the Black community during the Civil War. The SDP's position was founded on the state-rights argument that states can determine how a federal law is implemented within the state.

Therefore, the HBCUs needed to reestablish a political balance within the state legislatures to protect the rights of the Black population from the practice of racial discrimination, which systemically denied their rights at the state level or local level. The HBCUs could not regain the political balance that existed during the Reconstruction era because their funding was determined by state legislatures and organizations whose funding was jeopardized by taking political stances. Nevertheless, the HBCU students found a source of power they could use to restore the balance.

3.2 The Student Nonviolent Revolution

The HBCU educational network created an environment that encouraged the development of student nonviolent civil disobedience strategies, ultimately defeating the legal practice of racial discrimination in the South and across the United States. This defeat was manifested by the passage of the Great Society legislation enacted in the 1960s, which aimed to conclusively address the social and economic issues of inequality rooted in the practices of slave labor and racial discrimination in the United States.

These student-led nonviolent direct action strategies against racial discrimination occurred in the Southern cities that nurtured the largest concentration of HBCU students. The cities of Atlanta, Georgia; Montgomery, Alabama; Greensboro, North Carolina; Jackson, Mississippi; Nashville, Tennessee; and Baton Rouge, Louisiana, were the locations of the most dramatic and courageous student nonviolent civil disobedience campaigns against the practice of racial discrimination in the 1960s. These cities are home to Morehouse College (1867), Alabama State University (1867), North Carolina A&T (1891), Bennett College (1873), Tougaloo College (1869), Jackson State University (1877), Fisk University (1866), and Southern University (1880).

One of the iconic moments in civil rights history tied to HBCUs is the Montgomery Bus Boycott, which began on the campus of Alabama State University. Like a thumbprint invisible to the naked eye, HBCUs left their mark on each protest, march, and sit-in during the civil rights movement.

In December 1949, Jo Ann Robinson, an English professor at Alabama State University, boarded a bus in Montgomery, Alabama, paid her fare, and noticed two other passengers—a white woman seated in the third row and a Black man sitting near the back. Aware of the segregation laws that prohibited Black patrons from sitting in the whites-only section at the front of the bus, Robinson chose a seat in the middle.

The driver pulled over, walked back to where she was seated, and yelled at her, saying she was sitting too close to the white section. Fearing that he might hit her, Robinson fled the bus, feeling humiliated, embarrassed, and determined to mobilize against bus segregation.

When the Montgomery mayor and city council refused her demand to end the separation of races on city buses, she conceived the idea of a boycott. But activists in the Black community feared harsh reprisals—arrests, violence, and job losses for people who challenged the legal practice of racial discrimination supported by most Southern states.

Meanwhile, more Black bus riders began to experience similar abuse. Among the indignities, they were forced to pay at the front of the bus, then exit and reenter through a separate door leading to the Black section in the back. Occasionally, drivers would pull away before they could reenter, even though they had paid their fare.

The Montgomery NAACP secretary, Rosa Parks, already well known in the community for her efforts to achieve racial justice, on December 1, 1955, took a seat in the whites-only section during a bus ride and was arrested. Robinson, who had patiently waited for the right moment to implement her boycott plans, seized the opportunity.

With the help of students and other staff at Alabama State University, where she served as an English professor, Robinson prepared and mimeographed over 50,000 flyers, distributing them to Black city residents and urging them to stay off the buses for one day to protest Parks' arrest. Few, if anyone, imagined that the Montgomery Bus Boycott would last 13 months and bring about such a historic change.

On May 17, 1954, a team of HBCU-trained lawyers from Howard University, including Thurgood Marshall, who was eventually appointed to the Supreme Court, presented the *Brown v. Board of Education* case before the U.S. Supreme Court. This landmark case challenged the constitutionality of racial segregation in public schools.

The case was brought by Oliver Brown, who filed a class-action lawsuit against the Board of Education of Topeka, Kansas, after his daughter, Linda Brown, was denied entrance to an all-white elementary school. The lawsuit argued that the segregation of public schools based on race violated the Equal Protection Clause of the Fourteenth Amendment.

The case challenged the "separate but equal" doctrine established by the 1896 Supreme Court decision in *Plessy v. Ferguson*, which had allowed state-sponsored segregation if the separate facilities were purportedly equal. The Supreme Court, in a unanimous decision, ruled that racial segregation in public schools was unconstitutional.

The Court held that "separate educational facilities are inherently unequal" and that segregation violated the Equal Protection Clause of the Fourteenth Amendment. The *Brown v. Board of Education* case is considered one of the most important rulings in the history of the U.S. Supreme Court and a significant milestone in the fight for civil rights.

The decision was a significant victory for the Civil Rights Movement and set a precedent for future rulings against segregation and discrimination. It led to the desegregation of public schools across the United States, although the process was met with resistance in many areas, like Little Rock, Arkansas.

On September 2, 1957, the day before the schools were to open in Little Rock, Arkansas governor Orval Faubus appeared on statewide television to announce his intention to use the Arkansas National Guard troops to prevent the nine Black students from entering the all-white Central High School despite the 1954 United States Supreme Court ruling in *Brown v. the Board of Education of Topeka*, making segregated school illegal.

Four minutes away from Central High School's action, Philander Smith College, an HBCU in Little Rock, Arkansas, opened its doors to the "Little Rock Nine" to help them prepare for their first days as students after being turned away by the Arkansas National Guard. Philander Smith College was established in 1877 to provide educational opportunities for formerly enslaved people following the Civil War.

The school opened under the supervision of the Freedmen's Aid Society of the Methodist Episcopal Church and was named Walden Seminary to produce preachers and teachers. In 1882, Adeline Smith, widow of Philander Smith, an Illinois philanthropist, donated $10,500 to Walden Seminary, and the school's trustees renamed Philander Smith College to recognize this gift. Philander Smith College awarded its first baccalaureate degree in 1888. It became accredited by the North Central Association of Colleges and Schools in 1949, five years before being thrust into the Little Rock Nine Crisis in 1957.

The governor's order barring the students from entering the all-white Central High School would last two weeks. To prevent the Nine from falling behind in their coursework, Philander Smith College faculty members aided them while the NAACP and the school board pursued the matter through the federal courts.

During this time, the faculty provided tutorial opportunities for the students to enable them to stay current with their studies and rejoin their white classmates. The NAACP screened these students for their ability to withstand this ordeal, but few expected the violent reaction to the enrollment of these nine high school students.

A federal judge ordered the Arkansas National Guard removed on September 20, 1957, and the Little Rock Police Department took over to maintain order. The police escorted the nine Black students into the school on September 23, 1957, through an angry mob of some 1,000 white protesters gathered outside. Amid the ensuing rioting, the police removed the nine students.

The following day, President Eisenhower sent 1,200 members of the U.S. Army's 101st Airborne Division from Fort Campbell, Kentucky, and placed them in charge of the 10,000 Arkansas National Guardsmen on duty. Escorted by the troops, the Little Rock Nine attended their first full day of classes on September 25, 1957.

In February 1960, the Greensboro Four started lunch counter protests, or sit-ins, against racial discrimination in Greensboro, North Carolina. The sit-ins were organized by HBCU students at North Carolina Agricultural and Technical State University and the all-women's Bennett College. Their success led to national media coverage and lunch counter protests staged in cities nationwide.

Ezell Blair, Franklin McCain, Joseph McNeil, and David Richmond organized the sit-in to draw attention to racial segregation in the private sector. Aided by Ralph Johns, a local white businessman sympathetic to their cause, the students, dubbed the Greensboro Four, planned their civil disobedience in detail.

On the afternoon of February 1, 1960, the Greensboro Four entered Woolworth's general merchandise store with a dining area. The men bought small items and retained the receipt as proof of purchase before sitting down at the store's lunch counter.

While Black people were allowed to patronize the dining area, they were relegated to a standing snack bar, as the owners designated the lunch counters for "whites only." The Greensboro Four politely requested service at the counter, remaining seated while the waitstaff refused their orders.

The lunch counter manager contacted the police, but Johns had already alerted the local media. The police arrived, only to declare they could do nothing because the four men were paying customers of the store and had not taken any provocative actions.

The media response was immediate, as photos of the Greensboro Four appeared in local newspapers. The following day, the Greensboro Four returned to Woolworth's lunch counter, accompanied by twenty other Black university students.

The scene played out again on February 3 to 4, 1960, with protestors filling all the available seats and spilling out of the store onto the sidewalk outside. Within weeks, dining facilities across the South started to integrate, and by July 1960, the lunch counter at Greensboro Woolworths was serving Black patrons. The Greensboro sit-in provided a template for nonviolent resistance and marked an early success for the civil rights movement.

In April 1960, the Student Nonviolent Coordinating Committee (SNCC) was founded at a conference at Shaw University in Raleigh, North Carolina, by the students who led the sit-ins at segregated lunch counters in Greensboro, North Carolina, and Nashville, Tennessee. Prominent leaders who emerged from SNCC included John Lewis (Fisk University), Julian Bond (Morehouse College), Diane Nash (Fisk University), and Stokely Carmichael (Howard University).

SNCC played a crucial role in the Civil Rights Movement by coordinating and assisting direct-action challenges to racial discrimination. It was known for its commitment to nonviolence and participatory democracy and was instrumental in organizing voter registration drives, freedom rides, and other forms of protest across the Deep South.

On May 4, 1961, the Freedom Riders began with two buses departing from Washington, D.C., led by James Farmer, a Wiley College and Howard University graduate and founder of the Congress of Racial Equality (CORE). The riders aimed to travel through the Deep South, ultimately reaching New Orleans, to challenge the nonenforcement of Supreme Court decisions that declared segregation in interstate bus travel unconstitutional.

They aimed to ensure bus terminals, restrooms, and other facilities adhered to desegregation laws. By facing violent opposition, they hoped to compel the federal government to enforce civil rights laws and draw national and international attention to the civil rights struggle in the South.

Throughout the Freedom Rides, 436 individuals participated in at least 60 separate rides. However, due to the violent resistance they faced, not all riders completed the journey. The initial group encountered violence in South Carolina, but in Alabama, the reaction was much more severe.

On May 14, upon stopping outside Anniston to change a slashed tire, one bus was firebombed, and the Freedom Riders were beaten. Arriving in Birmingham, Alabama, the second bus was similarly attacked and the passengers beaten. In both cases, law enforcement was suspiciously late in responding, and there were suspicions of collusion in that late response.

Although the original Riders could not find a bus line to carry them farther, a second group of ten, originating in Nashville and partly organized by the Student Nonviolent Coordinating Committee (SNCC), renewed the effort. Undeterred by being arrested in Birmingham and transported back to Tennessee, the new Freedom Riders returned to Birmingham and, at the behest of U.S. Attorney General Robert F. Kennedy, secured a bus and protection from the State Highway Patrol as they traveled to Montgomery, Alabama, where, when local police failed to protect them, they were again beaten.

Afterward, National Guard support was provided when twenty-seven Freedom Riders traveled to Jackson, Mississippi, only to be arrested and jailed. On May 29, Kennedy ordered the Interstate Commerce Commission to enforce stricter guidelines banning segregation in interstate travel. Nevertheless, Freedom Riders continued to travel by public transportation in the South until that directive took effect in September. Despite the challenges, the Freedom Rides highlighted the need for federal enforcement of desegregation laws and played a crucial role in the Civil Rights Movement.

In the summer of 1964, SNCC undertook a pivotal American Civil Rights Movement campaign, the Mississippi Summer Project, also called Freedom Summer. It aimed to increase voter registration among Black Americans in Mississippi, a state notorious for its severe racial discrimination. College students were recruited and trained to register Mississippi Black voters during the summer before the 1964 presidential election.

The SNCC voter registration campaign was led by Bob Moses, a key organizer for SNCC who was instrumental in organizing the student segment of the campaign, and Fannie Lou Hamer, a SNCC organizer and Mississippi civil rights activist, who played a significant role in mobilizing the local community.

Volunteers, including many white college students from the North, traveled to Mississippi to assist Black Americans in registering to vote. Freedom Schools were established in rural Mississippi counties to provide education and promote political awareness among the Black community and encourage them to register to vote.

The campaign faced severe backlash from the white Mississippi political power structure, which viewed it as a threat to their political dominance. Their opposition to the voter registration campaign included the murder of three civil rights workers—James Chaney, Andrew Goodman, and Michael Schwerner. The campaign drew national attention to the struggles encountered by Black communities in the South and helped pave the way for the passage of the Voting Rights Act of 1965.

Despite the challenges, the campaign empowered local Black communities and laid the groundwork for future civil rights efforts. Freedom Summer was a courageous and transformative effort that significantly advanced the cause of civil rights in the United States.

On March 7, 1965, SNCC member John Lewis played a crucial role in the events surrounding the march across the Edmund Pettus Bridge, also known as "Bloody Sunday." SNCC sent two teams to Selma, Alabama, which became emblematic of the fight to secure Black voting rights and the involvement of HBCUs in the 1965 marches, marking a turning point in that struggle.

Students and faculty from HBCUs, such as Alabama State University and Tuskegee University, were actively involved in that march. These institutions served as a base for organizing and mobilizing participants from Selma to Montgomery, Alabama.

For example, Alabama State University students planned the execution of the march, and the university served as a meeting point for activists. Additionally, many HBCU students and faculty members joined the march to show solidarity and support for the fight for voting rights.

These campaigns and others not listed here directly contributed to the passage of Great Society legislation, which finally provided the authority and funding necessary to enforce the rights granted by the Reconstruction Amendments. These rights include the protection of U.S. citizenship, the right to vote, and the prohibition of racial discrimination in every state. This legislation, akin to the Reconstruction Act of 1867, resulted in the election of Black officials who could hold federal, state, and local governments accountable for the devastating impact of racial discrimination on the economic development of the Black community.

After multiple revisions by several presidential administrations, the tools provided in the original Great Society legislation are even more helpful for finishing the work started by the HBCU educational network in building economically competitive Black communities. Now is the time for these institutions to use these tools and finish building the economically prosperous Black communities in the South that the legal practice of racial discrimination impeded after the end of Reconstruction.

HBCU students were the vanguard of the Civil Rights Movement of the 1960s, which led to the passage of the Great Society legislation that required the federal government to finally enforce the fundamental rights outlined in the Reconstruction Amendments of the U.S. Constitution of the 1860s. These students employed revolutionary nonviolent civil disobedience strategies formulated on HBCU campuses and specifically designed to challenge racial discrimination in the Southern states to achieve their goal.

However, as stated in the words of a 1971 poem by Gil Scott-Heron, "The Revolution Will Not Be Televised," the nonviolent student revolutionaries' actions, which aired on television during evening news shows and between commercial breaks, were not the revolution.

Their actions expanded the meaning of the phrase, 'all men are created equal,' contained in the American Declaration of Independence, to include differences due to race, color, religion, sex (including gender identity and sexual orientation), national origin, age, disability, or genetic information. Still, these actions were not the revolution.

The revolution occurred in the minds of the HBCU students and eventually the American people to believe in what seemed impossible.

3.3 Black Bird Fly into the Light

HBCU participants in the Civil Rights Movement supported policy changes in the Great Society legislation to end legal racial discrimination nationwide. President Lyndon Baines Johnson (LBJ) of Texas, one of the states of the old Confederacy, signed the legislation into law. The legislation also included the HBCU designation, which created a federal funding opportunity for these higher education institutions.

This designation marked a significant turning point in the operations of HBCUs that had no relation to the possibility of federal funding. The implementation of the Great Society legislation transformed the practice of racial discrimination in the South by allowing Black students to enroll in predominantly white institutions (PWIs) and expanding college enrollment opportunities for the Black college-age population.

Before LBJ's landmark legislation, Black college students could attend certain PWIs in the North. Following the bill, the federal government was obligated to uphold Black college students' rights and wishes to enroll in the college of their choice, including those in the South.

These policy changes increased equality in educational opportunities for the Black college-age population and led to a surge in college enrollment. This surge in college enrollment was one of, if not the greatest, accomplishments of the Civil Rights Movement. It initiated a trend of prosperity for Black people that continues today.

This growth results from HBCU students' demands through active protests on behalf of the Black community for the Great Society legislation. However, the other significant impact shown in the data is the end of HBCUs' marketplace monopoly on the education of Black students.

Figure 3.1 shows that the most dramatic enrollment increases occurred between 1960 and 1975 during the implementation of the Civil Rights Movement and the Great Society legislation. Total Black college student enrollment went from 100,000 to 1,032,000, and HBCU enrollment more than doubled from 60,000 to 150,000 during this period.

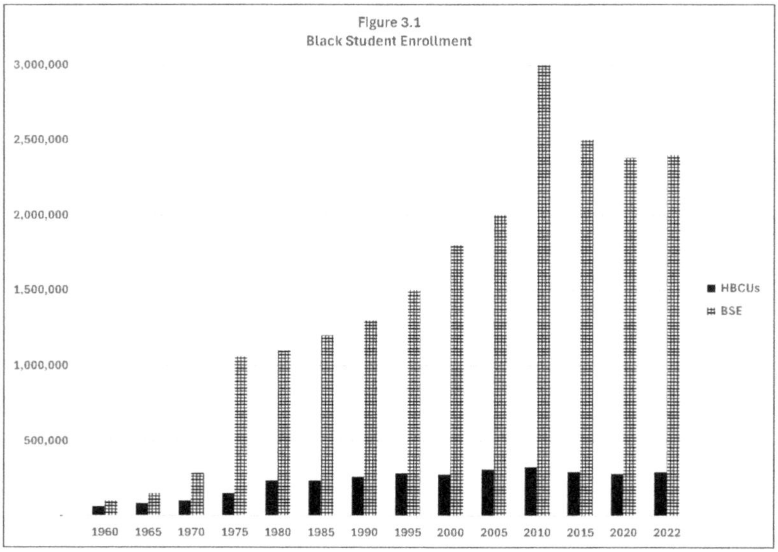

FIGURE 3.1 Black student enrollment

The data show an enrollment of 100,000 Black college students in 1960, 2,400,000 Black college students in 2022, and an increase in HBCU enrollment from 60,000 in 1960 to 282,000 in 2022.

Figure 3.1 illustrates that overall HBCU and Black enrollment increased during this period; however, the percentage of Black students attending HBCUs decreased compared to PWIs. The policy changes advocated by HBCU students in the 1960s contributed significantly to the growth in educational attainment among Black college students.

However, the policy changes benefiting Black college-age students exceeded HBCUs' capacity to meet the demand for a college education among Black college-age students. Before the policy changes, 60 percent of enrolled Black college students attended HBCUs in 1960; in 2022, only 12 percent attended HBCUs, highlighting the need for HBCUs to compete for the education of Black students.

These policy changes drastically altered the practice of racial discrimination in the South and provided educational opportunities, civil rights, voting rights, housing rights, and economic growth for the Black community. The Great Society programs enforced Blacks' right to attend PWIs and encouraged college attendance in general by assisting students in funding college education based on their family's income level.

These statistics show that HBCU efforts against the practice of institutional racism encouraged Black students to attend college, and a more sizable portion of those students chose PWIs. However, HBCUs did not lose their dominance or ability as the leaders in the effort to eliminate the practice of institutional racial discrimination in the United States.

HBCUs remain as crucial as ever, serving as centers of education, cultural heritage, and community support. They preserve the rich history of Black culture and continue to pave the way for generations of Black students to pursue higher education and achieve their academic and career goals.

Figure 3.2 illustrates that, before the passage of the Great Society legislation in 1965, approximately 60 percent of Black college students attended HBCUs, and 5 percent of the Black college-age population were enrolled in college. The data show how the passage of this legislation affected enrollment at HBCUs and among the Black college-age population.

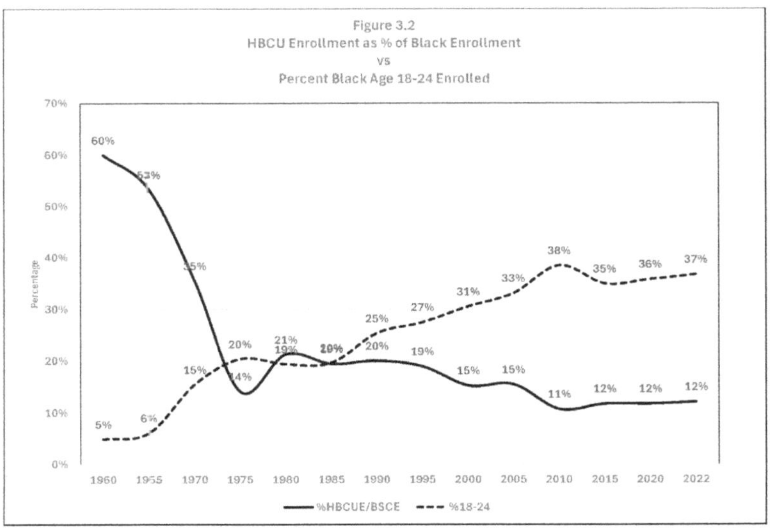

FIGURE 3.2 HBCU enrollment as percent of Black enrollment versus percent Black age 18 to 24 enrolled

This trend, started by the Great Society legislation, stimulated overall college student enrollment by providing grants and loans to fund college tuition based on family household income. This legislation and the overall increase in Black family income during this decade allowed Black families to send their children to college in even greater numbers.

By the end of the 1970s, Black student and HBCU enrollment were on a growth pattern that extended into 2022 at an average annual growth rate of 20 percent per decade. As a result, the percentage of the Black college-age population 18 to 24 attending college improved to 37 percent in 2022 compared to 5percent of the Black college-age population in 1960.

The rise in college enrollment among the Black college-age population after the Civil Rights Movement profoundly impacted the economic development of the Black community. The increase in college enrollment led to a significant rise in educational attainment within the Black community, providing access to better-paying jobs and careers that required higher education.

Higher education enabled Black individuals to pursue broader opportunities, including white-collar positions. By 1970, approximately 10 percent of Black individuals were enrolled in college, marking a threefold increase from pre-WWII figures. This trend continued, leading to more Black men and women holding professional and managerial positions.

Increased access to higher education facilitated upward economic mobility, resulting in higher wages and improved job prospects, contributing to the Black community's overall financial stability and growth. Educated individuals are reinvested in their communities, contributing to local economic development. This reinvestment includes starting businesses, participating in local governance, and supporting community initiatives.

While disparities still existed, progress in educational attainment and employment opportunities helped reduce poverty rates within the Black community. Overall, the increase in college enrollment among the Black population after the Civil Rights Movement played a crucial role in enhancing economic development and improving the quality of life within the Black community.

The Great Society Legislation ushered in by the Civil Rights Movement had an overall positive impact on the Black community but not necessarily on the financial position of HBCUs and their surrounding communities. The legislation included the enforcement of fair housing practices, allowing Black families to move into neighborhoods previously restricted due to racial discrimination.

Figure 3.2 shows divergent patterns, with a larger percentage of the Black college-age population attending PWIs and a smaller percentage attending HBCUs. This same pattern is observable in Black household data for the same period.

In 1960, an estimated 50 percent to 60 percent of Black households lived in predominantly Black neighborhoods, while in 2020, that percentage has significantly decreased to around 20 percent to 30 percent of Black households residing in predominantly Black areas. The data show how Black households benefited from fair housing legislation that allowed them to seek better housing opportunities outside of the historically Black communities to which they were confined before the passage of the fair housing laws.

This pattern represented the second Great Migration, as Black households left the communities that supported and surrounded the HBCUs for better homes and lifestyles made possible by the passage of the Great Society Legislation. What remained were the HBCU campuses and the households unable to take advantage of the opportunities provided by the fair housing laws contained in the legislation.

Despite the divergent patterns shown in Figure 3.2, the growth in Black college student enrollment and HBCU enrollment represents an opportunity for HBCUs to play a leading role in the recovery of Black communities. HBCUs were a successful investment, providing the economic base that allowed the South to transition from an economy driven by slave labor into an economy driven by free labor.

This investment is still in place, and the legal practice of racial discrimination, which limited its return, was eliminated during the one hundred years between 1865 and 1965. This one-hundred-year struggle produced the freedom needed to allow Black communities to function competitively in the free market and begin the accumulation of family generational wealth.

The Black community earned the Great Society legislation programs and policies, and the involvement of HBCU students played a leading role in the final years of a hundred years of struggle. The elements of these hard-earned freedoms can help rebuild HBCUs and support the families of the formerly enslaved in all the old Confederate states.

It is now time for the administrators of HBCUs to take the next step and complete their original mission: to enhance the lives of the Black community. Now is the time to leverage this investment and finish building the Black community development impeded by violence and the legal practice of racial discrimination.

CHAPTER 4

How We Finally Got Over

4.1 Making a Way Out of No Way

In his 1963 book *Why We Can't Wait*, Dr. Martin Luther King, Jr., an HBCU graduate of Morehouse College, explores the events and forces that led to the success of the Civil Rights Movement. In recognition of the movement's success, he proposed that the U.S. Congress pass a Bill of Rights for the Disadvantaged to compensate the Black population of the United States for the sacrifices they were forced to make on behalf of the nation as the direct victims of slavery.

In addition, his proposal extended these compensations to all poor Americans whose economic conditions were the derivative victims of slavery. The involuntary servitude of the Black man cheapened the value of all labor in the U.S. labor market and depressed the wage rate structure and earning potential of labor.

His proposed Bill of Rights for the Disadvantaged was modeled after the Servicemen's Readjustment Act, better known as the GI Bill of Rights. President Franklin D. Roosevelt signed the GI Bill of Rights into law on June 22, 1944, to compensate American veterans returning home after serving their country during World War II.

The American military forces received payment for participating in the war effort and were obligated to serve. The GI Bill of Rights was additional compensation for veterans who sacrificed significantly by serving their nation. It helped them transition financially back into civilian life by offsetting the economic losses incurred for voluntarily providing their services to the U.S. military.

The bill's compensation included funds for veterans to attend college, vocational schools, and other educational institutions. This included tuition, books, and living expenses, making higher education accessible to millions of veterans.

The bill provided veterans with federally guaranteed loans to purchase homes, farms, and businesses. This significantly increased homeownership among veterans and contributed to the postwar housing boom. Veterans also received up to one year of unemployment compensation while they searched for jobs. This safety net assisted them in transitioning back into civilian life.

The GI Bill established hospitals and provided medical care for veterans, ensuring they had access to necessary health services. Veterans could also obtain low-interest loans to start businesses, fostering entrepreneurship and economic growth. These benefits helped millions of veterans reintegrate into civilian life, pursue higher education, achieve homeownership, and contribute to the postwar economic boom.

In his book, Dr. King proposed that the Bill of Rights for the Disadvantaged contain a compensation structure like the benefits of the GI Bill. He concluded that such a measure was the best way to offset the debilitating economic impact of involuntary servitude on those directly impacted and for the indirect effect on the U.S. labor force.

According to Dr. King, involuntary servitude was a direct, significant sacrifice made by Black people that was ultimately responsible for building the United States and Western European nations into dominant economic world powers—such a sacrifice required recognition through readjustment benefits like those provided to the returning veterans.

In addition, Dr. King proposed that benefits should not be limited to those who directly made the sacrifice of involuntary servitude but should be available to all poor and disadvantaged Americans due to the derivative impact of involuntary servitude on the wage structure of the labor market. The bill would help the Black and poor white population of the United States reintegrate into economic life after the adverse financial impact of involuntary servitude on the wage rate structure.

Dr. King also alluded to the idea of providing the Black population with direct monetary payments to offset the economic damage caused by slavery. Although he never used the term reparations, Dr. King concluded that the amount owed to the formerly enslaved, if accurately calculated, would exceed the capacity of the U.S. government treasury and lead to economic ruin for both the nation and the entire Western European economy.

The work of Eric Williams, a prominent Trinidadian historian and politician, supports the logic behind Dr. King's calculations. Williams was born on September 25, 1911, in Port of Spain, Trinidad, and died on March 29, 1981. He is best known for being the first prime minister of Trinidad and Tobago, serving from 1962 until he died in 1981.

He founded the People's National Movement (PNM) in 1956 and led the country to independence from British colonial rule in 1962. For his significant contributions to Trinidad and Tobago's political and social development, Williams is often called the "Father of the Nation."

In his book *Capitalism and Slavery*, published in 1944, Williams presents a compelling quantitative argument about the economic foundations of slavery and its role in developing Western capitalism. This argument supports the logic behind Dr. King's position on direct payment for the damage caused by the slave trade. Williams argues that the primary motivation for the transatlantic slave trade and the use of enslaved labor in the Americas was economic.

The profits generated from the slave trade and the American plantation system were crucial in funding the Industrial Revolution in Britain and America. The wealth accumulated from the slave trade and the exploitation of enslaved Africans provided investments in industries such as shipbuilding, manufacturing, textiles, finance, and the capital necessary for the Industrial Revolution.

In addition, the most significant factor in the abolition of slavery was the decline of the profitability of the slave economy rather than moral or humanitarian concerns. As industrial capitalism grew, the economic benefits of slavery diminished, leading to its eventual abolition in Britain and America.

The book highlights how the wealth generated from slavery contributed to the growth of major British cities and industries. It also underscores the global economy's interconnectedness, with the slave trade linking Europe, Africa, and the Americas. Williams' work influenced the understanding of the economic dimensions of slavery and its lasting impact on global financial systems, as well as Dr. King's position on reparations, which, like the word reparations, were not included in Dr. King's book.

Ultimately, the passage of the Great Society legislation is what the Civil Rights Movement accomplished to offset the adverse economic and social effects of 250 years of chattel slavery in the United States. Upon closer examination, this legislation contained and has continued to evolve into most of the components of Dr. King's Bill of Rights for the Disadvantaged.

The Great Society legislation is a series of domestic programs launched by President Lyndon B. Johnson in the 1960s to eliminate poverty and racial injustice, called the War on Poverty. Some key pieces of legislation that comprise the Great Society are:

The Civil Rights Act of 1964 prohibited discrimination based on race, color, religion, sex, or national origin in employment practices and public accommodations.

The Economic Opportunity Act of 1964 created programs such as Job Corps, VISTA (Volunteers in Service to America), and Head Start to combat poverty by providing education, job training, and community development.

The Voting Rights Act of 1965 aimed to eliminate racial discrimination in voting by prohibiting literacy tests and other discriminatory practices that had been used to disenfranchise Black Americans.

The Elementary and Secondary Education Act of 1965 provided federal funding to improve educational opportunities in public schools, particularly those serving low-income students.

Social Security Amendments of 1965 established Medicare and Medicaid, providing health insurance for the elderly and low-income individuals.

The Higher Education Act of 1965 increased federal funding for colleges and universities, provided financial assistance to students, and aimed to make higher education more accessible.

The Immigration and Nationality Act of 1965 abolished the national origins quota system, which had restricted immigration from certain countries. It established a new immigration policy to reunite immigrant families and attract skilled labor.

The National Endowment for the Arts and Humanities Act of 1965 created the National Endowment for the Arts (NEA) and the National Endowment for the Humanities (NEH) to support cultural and educational projects.

The Fair Housing Act of 1968 prohibited discrimination in the sale, rental, and financing of housing based on race, color, religion, sex, or national origin and created the Department of Housing and Urban Development (HUD).

Every component of the Great Society legislation was preceded by a direct act of nonviolent civil disobedience designed to focus the attention of the U.S. political system and the public on the discriminatory denial of the fundamental civil rights of the Black population in the United States.

The following list is not intended to be a definitive chronology of every event during the one-hundred-year struggle from 1865 to 1965 that led up to the enforcement of the Reconstruction Amendments to the U.S. Constitution on behalf of its Black population. It includes some pivotal moments in the Civil Rights Movement that were supported by HBCU students and influenced the passage of the Great Society legislation of the 1960s.

The Civil Rights Act of July 2, 1964, was preceded by:

- The *Brown v. Board of Education* Case—May 17, 1954
- Montgomery Bus Boycott—December 5, 1955
- The Little Rock Nine—September 2, 1957
- The Greensboro Four—February 1, 1960
- The Freedom Rides—May 4, 1961
- The March on Washington—August 28, 1963
- The Mississippi Summer Project—June 15, 1964

The Voting Rights Act of August 6, 1965, was preceded by:

- The Selma to Montgomery Marches—March 7, 1965

The Fair Housing Act of April 11, 1968, was preceded by:

- The Memphis Sanitation Strike—February 12, 1968

There is no direct cause and effect implied here because Black people committed numerous acts of nonviolent civil disobedience during U.S. history, declaring their opposition to the practice of slavery.

Still, these specific nonviolent civil disobedience actions, greatly influenced by HBCU-related participation and the support of the Black community, preceded the passage of the Great Society legislation. These actions gained the attention of the nation. They tilted political power to finally enable the Black community to renegotiate the terms of their involuntary servitude and participate in the generational accumulation of wealth denied to them due to the practice of legal discrimination in the United States.

These nonviolent acts of civil disobedience, listed above, were characteristic of the Civil Rights Movement, which gained widespread recognition. However, the movement's foundation and true essence are best captured by the stories presented in the works of Carter G. Woodson, particularly his 1922 book, *The Negro in Our History*, which was integrated into the curriculum of the HBCU educational network.

The book provided a comprehensive and accessible account of Black history, largely neglected or misrepresented in mainstream historical narratives. It became a crucial educational resource for schools and colleges, helping to fill the Black history education gap. By documenting the contributions and achievements of Black Americans throughout history, Woodson's work instilled a sense of pride and identity within the Black community.

The meticulous research and scholarship in Woodson's stories challenged the prevailing stereotypes and misconceptions about Black Americans. His work corrected historical inaccuracies and provided a more balanced and truthful account of Black history. The book laid the groundwork for future historians and scholars to build upon, inspiring further research and writing on Black American history and contributing to the development of the field.

The work led to the Black History Month which originated from Negro History Week, which was established by Woodson and the Association for the Study of Negro Life and History (ASNLH; now the Association for the Study of African American Life and History [ASALH]), in 1926. Woodson chose the second week of February to coincide with the birthdays of Abraham Lincoln and Frederick Douglass. The week-long celebration aimed to promote the achievements of Americans of African descent. Over time, the event grew in popularity and significance, eventually expanding to a month-long celebration in 1976.

Most importantly, Woodson believed understanding and appreciating Black history was essential for achieving racial equality. His book was part of his broader efforts to promote the study of Black history to combat the legal practice of racial discrimination. This history was taught to HBCU students, and they taught it to their students, which was a source of hope that fueled the HBCU education network's work in preparing the Black community to compete equally in a free market economy, to figure out how to gain the opportunity to compete, and to use the opportunities gained to start the accumulation of generational wealth for the Black community.

How do you make a way out of no way? You rely on faith to overcome a seemingly impossible situation or dilemma. In Hebrews 11:1, faith is "the assurance of things hoped for, the conviction of things not seen," meaning it firmly trusts a certainty about unseen realities.

History is an unseen reality that, if known and understood, can provide the certainty needed to have faith in achieving what appears to be impossible outcomes, such as the 1960 Black vote that proved essential in the election of President Kennedy and led to the 1964 Black support of LBJ, who included the MLK's Bill of Rights for the Disadvantaged in the Great Society legislation.

4.2 Economic Mobility

The HBCU educational network helped the U.S. Black population transition from enslavement to freedom and became the foundation for the development of free Black communities. At the same time, this network and these communities were gaining the knowledge needed to start the accumulation of generational wealth by working to end the legal practice of racial discrimination in the United States.

The struggle to overcome the adverse effects of racial discrimination by HBCUs led directly to improving the economic status of the Black community as well as the U.S. economy. The legal practice of racial discrimination is the primary reason for the disparity that exists between the poverty rates and income level of the Black household and the average household in the United States, as shown in Figures 4.1 and 4.2.

While the disparities remain, the data from 1959 to 2023 shows that the turning point in the economic performance of the Black community occurred in the 1960s and 1970s. This coincided with the passage of the 1960s Great Society legislation, which included provisions to enforce equal protection under the law for the Black community and was meant to offset the negative economic impact of the legal practice of racial discrimination for decades.

Title VII of the Civil Rights Act of 1964, part of the Great Society legislation, had a profound impact on employment practices in the United States and the drop in the poverty level of the Black community shown in Figure 4.1, especially between 1960 and 1970, but also beyond. The Act outlawed employment discrimination based on race, color, religion, sex, or national origin. This was a significant step toward creating a more equitable workplace and allowed the Black community access to higher-paying jobs in the Southern states, where most of them lived.

The Act established the Equal Employment Opportunity Commission (EEOC) to enforce federal laws prohibiting employment discrimination. The EEOC was empowered to investigate complaints, mediate disputes, and bring lawsuits against employers who violated the law. This led to numerous landmark court cases that further defined and expanded the scope of employment discrimination laws.

The Act helped shift societal attitudes toward discrimination and equality. It promoted the idea that employment decisions should be based on merit rather than personal characteristics, the opposite of racial discrimination, which dominated employment decisions in the South before the Act was passed.

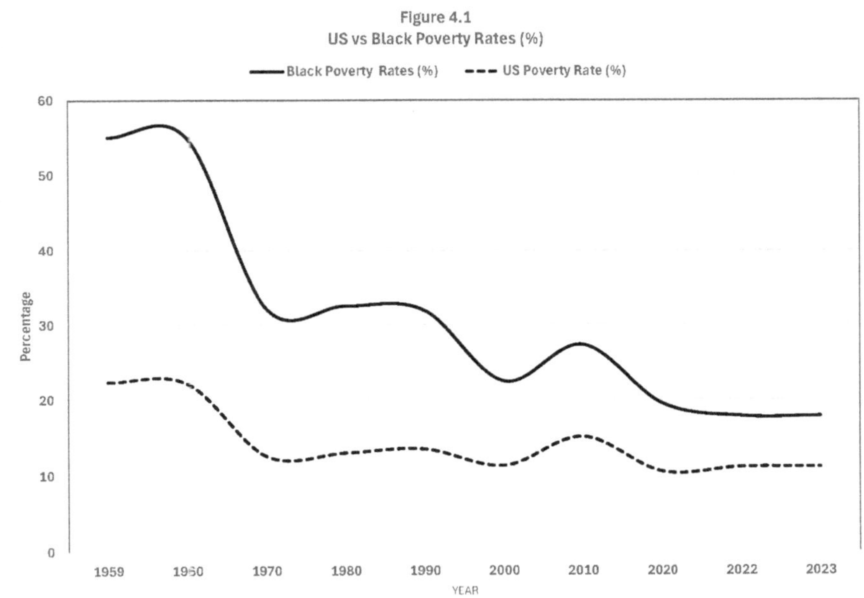

FIGURE 4.1 U.S. versus Black poverty rates (percent)

Despite progress, challenges remain, and the Equal Employment Opportunity Act of 1972 was passed to strengthen and expand the enforcement of civil rights laws in the workplace. Many employers continued discriminatory practices, and stronger measures were needed to ensure compliance. The 1972 Act extended the coverage of anti-discrimination laws to include more employers, including state and local governments, educational institutions, and labor organizations. This broadened the scope of protections for workers and job opportunities for the Black labor force, which was systemically excluded from these job opportunities.

The Act granted the Equal Employment Opportunity Commission (EEOC) greater authority to enforce anti-discrimination laws. This included the power to file lawsuits against employers who violated the law, which was a significant step in holding employers accountable.

The Act sought to create a fair and equal employment environment, ensuring that all individuals could earn a living for their families based on their abilities and qualifications rather than being hindered by discriminatory practices. These measures were essential in promoting equal employment opportunities and addressing the systemic legal practice of discrimination within the U.S. labor market.

The passage of these Acts corresponds to a rise in Black and U.S. median household income, as shown in Figure 4.2, from the 1960s and beyond. The underlying data show that the increase in Black household incomes significantly boosts U.S. median household income growth.

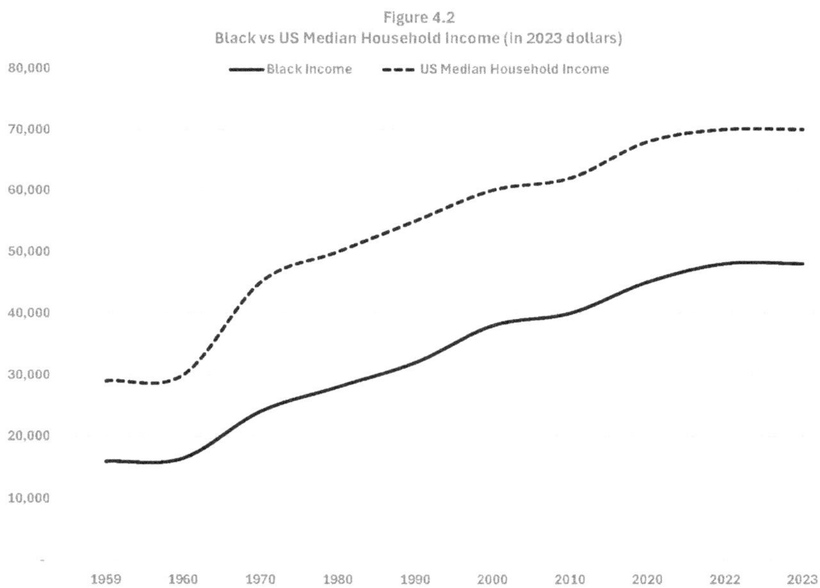

FIGURE 4.2 Black versus U.S. median household income (in 2023 dollars)

However, the increases shown could not have occurred without a labor force waiting and ready with the skills needed to take advantage of equal employment opportunities. HBCUs were created to educate and prepare a previously enslaved and illiterate Black labor force to take advantage of the job opportunities created by the Great Society legislation's attack on discrimination in the job market.

HBCUs were the lead institutions in building the educational network—prekindergarten, kindergarten, elementary, middle school, and high school—needed to equip the Black labor force with the skills to compete in a free market economy. HBCUs educated the students who became this educational network's staff, faculty, and administrators.

HBCUs provided access to higher education for many Black students who might not have had the opportunity otherwise. They consistently conferred a significant percentage of bachelor's degrees to Black students, particularly in STEM fields.

Graduates of HBCUs are more likely to move into higher-income quintiles compared to graduates of non-HBCUs. This upward mobility has been a critical factor in improving the economic status of the Black community.

HBCUs produced many Black professionals, including engineers, doctors, lawyers, and judges. These institutions are instrumental in building the Black middle class and fostering leadership within the community.

Today, HBCUs are often located in economically disadvantaged areas but have always had a significant positive impact on their local economies. They create jobs, support local businesses, and provide essential services to their communities.

HBCUs encourage entrepreneurship and business ownership among their students and alumni. They established programs and partnerships to support Black entrepreneurs, helping to close the revenue gap between Black-owned and non-Black-owned businesses.

HBCUs have also contributed to their students' and communities' physical health and well-being. Studies have shown that Black students who attend HBCUs are less likely to develop risk factors for chronic diseases later in life. The combined sacrifice of the HBCU students, staff, faculty, administration, and Black community participating in the Civil Rights Movement opened the doors to these economic opportunities.

Despite the apparent need to address the negative social and economic impact of racial discrimination, the War on Poverty has been subject to various misrepresentations. One common misrepresentation is that it was primarily about welfare. It encompassed multiple programs to improve education, healthcare, and employment opportunities.

Critics often claim that the War on Poverty failed because poverty still exists. However, the poverty rate significantly decreased from 19 percent in 1964 to 11.2 percent in 1974. The programs implemented had a substantial impact on reducing poverty, even if they did not eradicate it.

Some argue that the War on Poverty led to excessive government spending without results. While it did involve significant investment, many programs, such as Medicare and Medicaid, have provided essential services to millions of Americans.

There is a belief that the War on Poverty created a dependent culture. However, many initiatives, such as education and job training programs, were designed to provide opportunities for self-improvement and economic mobility. These misrepresentations often overlook the nuanced and multifaceted nature of the War on Poverty and its contributions to social and economic progress.

These pieces of legislation collectively improved the quality of life for all Americans by addressing issues of poverty, education, health care, and civil rights. Although the format differs from the GI Bill, the Great Society legislation contains most of the issues Dr. King championed in his book, written before the bill was formulated.

These domestic programs exceeded the scope of the GI Bill in terms of the types of benefits offered and the population segment that could receive them. The GI Bill was limited to veterans, while the Great Society programs were available to all Americans.

All Americans receive housing, employment, education, health care, business, food and income assistance, and community development benefits, which are components of the Great Society legislation still in place today. The legislative achievements contained in the Great Society domestic programs were a success by any measure, and like the GI Bill before it, they generated an economic boom.

Dr. King and the other HBCU graduates who worked in the struggle to acquire the freedom to allow the Black community to accumulate generational wealth were victorious. The provisions of the Great Society legislation profoundly affected the Black community's economic status, as the percentage of Black households living at or below the poverty level dropped from 55 percent to 17 percent, the most significant improvement experienced by any population segment of the nation.

Another significant improvement was among the poor white Americans because white Americans represent the most substantial number of every economic category of the nation's population. However, these same results were achieved for all poor households in the United States. Access to better jobs, education, and health care reduced the number of U.S. households living at or below the poverty level to 11 percent in 2023. It dramatically improved the economic condition of the Black population in the United States.

4.3 Marching Out of Poverty

The economic condition of the Black population in the United States has seen significant improvements from 1960 to 2023, as shown in Figures 4.1 and 4.2, which show poverty rates and median household income, respectively. The poverty rate for Black Americans has decreased from around 55 percent in 1960 to about 17 percent in 2023, and Black homeownership rates have increased from about 38 percent in 1960 to approximately 46 percent in 2023.

In 1960, the median household income for Black families was approximately $16,500 (adjusted to 2023 dollars). By 2023, this had increased to about $53,000. The Black unemployment rate has decreased significantly. In 1960, it was around 10.2 percent; in 2023, it was approximately 5.5 percent, a record low.

The Black labor force participation rate, which represents the percentage of the Black labor force that has jobs, has improved and is now comparable to that of the United States. As of November 2024, Black American individuals' labor force participation rate is 62.4 percent. In comparison, the overall U.S. labor force participation rate is 62.5 percent.

High school graduation rates for Black students have increased from about 25 percent in 1960 to over 90 percent in 2023. In 1960, the college enrollment rate for Black high school graduates was approximately 4.9 percent. By 2023, this rate had increased significantly to about 36 percent. College enrollment and graduation rates have grown substantially, contributing to better employment opportunities and higher incomes.

The HBCU educational network, extending from prekindergarten to higher education, is the dominant factor propelling the improvement in the educational attainment of the Black community and the accompanying economic improvements. However, HBCUs' involvement in the efforts to remove the barriers of racial discrimination from the job market made the most significant impact on the economic progress that occurred in the Black community.

In 1940, most Blacks lived in the South and on the land as laborers, farmers, and sharecroppers, and one in eight owned the land on which they worked. Five percent of Black men were engaged in nonmanual, white-collar work, and the other 95 percent held ill-paid, insecure, manual jobs that few whites would take, while 60 percent of Black women were employed as domestic servants.

Segregation in the South and discrimination in the North did create a sheltered market for some Black businesses and occupations, such as funeral homes, beauty parlors, and barber shops that served a Black community barred from patronizing "white" establishments. But the number was minuscule, so for the most part, the Black community was indeed trapped in a condition of economic poverty.

These conditions were best described in Gunnar Myrdal's book, *An American Dilemma: The Negro Problem and Modern Democracy*, published in 1944, which is a comprehensive study of race relations in the United States. Myrdal identified a fundamental conflict between the American ideals of justice and equality and the reality of racial discrimination against Black Americans. He termed this the "American dilemma."

Myrdal introduced the concept of cumulative causation, where poverty and discrimination perpetuate a cycle. He argued that improving the conditions of Black Americans would reduce prejudice, and reducing prejudice would improve their conditions.

Myrdal emphasized that the "Negro problem" was essentially a "white man's problem," as white Americans were responsible for the systemic disadvantages faced by Black Americans. He highlighted the importance of gaining publicity for the plight of Black Americans, noting that increased awareness was crucial for driving social change. The book influenced public opinion and policy, and it was cited in the landmark *Brown v. Board of Education* Supreme Court case, which declared racial segregation in public schools unconstitutional. Myrdal's work contributes significantly to understanding race relations and the ongoing struggle for racial equality in the United States.

Beginning in the 1940s, demographic and economic changes and a significant shift in white racial attitudes set Blacks on a path toward much greater equality. New Deal minimum wage legislation, which established minimum wages and hours, ended the practice of Southern employers hiring low-wage Black workers, further stifling industrial development in the region.

In addition, the trend toward mechanized agriculture and a diminished demand for American cotton in the face of international competition combined to displace Blacks from the land. With the shortage of workers in Northern manufacturing plants following the outbreak of World War II, Southern Blacks were in search of jobs, and they boarded trains and buses during a Great Migration that lasted through the mid-1960s.

They found what they were looking for: wages so strikingly high that in 1953, the average income for a Black family in the North was almost twice that of those who remained in the South. Throughout the 1950s, wages rose steadily, and unemployment was low.

A decade later, the gains were even more striking. From 1940 to 1970, Black men cut the income gap by about a third, and by 1970, they were earning (on average) roughly 60 percent of what white men earned. In subsequent years, these trends continued, although at a more leisurely pace.

For instance, today, more than 30 percent of Black men and nearly 60 percent of Black women hold white-collar jobs. In 1970, only 2.2 percent of American physicians were Black, but the figure is now 4.5 percent. However, while the percentage of

Black families with middle-class incomes rose almost 40 percent between 1940 and 1970, it has increased only 10 points since then.

This story of the tremendous economic progress made by the Black community since the start of the War on Poverty is largely overshadowed by negative stories about race and race relations. Because the media rarely reports on the facts regarding economic progress, the Black underclass continues to shape the perception of Black America in the eyes of much of the public. Many assume that Blacks live in ghettos, often in high-rise public housing projects, where crime and welfare checks are seen as their primary sources of income.

White as well as Black Americans hold this stereotype about the economic condition of the Black communities. Blacks are even more prone than whites to exaggerate the extent to which the Black community is trapped in inner-city poverty. Statistics from the Gallup poll show that about one-fifth of all whites, but almost half of Black respondents, said that at least three out of four Blacks are impoverished urban residents. And yet, Blacks who consider themselves to be middle class outnumber those with incomes below the poverty line by a wide margin.

In 1958, 44 percent of whites said they would move if a Black family became their next-door neighbor; today, the figure is 1 percent. In 1964, the year the Civil Rights Act was passed, only 18 percent of whites claimed to have a Black friend; today, 86 percent say they do, while 87 percent of Blacks assert they have white friends.

In 2023, over 50 percent of Black households consider themselves members of the middle class, and 46 percent own their own homes, a figure that rises to 75 percent if we look at Black married couples. Black two-parent families earn only 13percent less than those who are white, and almost a third of the Black population lives in suburbia.

Comparing economic data from 1960 to 2023 indicates that the HBCU educational network, for the most part, successfully equipped the Black community with the knowledge and skills needed to compete effectively in the PWI educational network and the free marketplace. The data analysis might even suggest these initiatives were so effective that one can conclude that HBCUs have completed their principal mission and can now ride off into the sunset.

However, there are economic and social disparities within the Black community directly on the other side of the black wrought iron gates that divide the HBCUs from their surrounding communities. The ongoing role of HBCUs in America is linked to their continued efforts to foster generational wealth in the census tract where they are located.

The economic and demographic data of the majority Black census tracts where HBCUs are located often show distinct differences from the average U.S. census tract. These census tracts that surround HBCUs have a higher percentage of Black or African American residents than the national average and a higher proportion of single-parent households. The age distribution in these census tracts tends to have a higher percentage of younger residents and fewer elderly residents compared to the national average.

The median household income in these census tracts is generally lower than the national average, while the poverty level is higher. Unemployment rates tend to exceed the national average, and employment is concentrated in a single industry. Homeownership rates are usually lower in these census tracts, with housing values and rental costs also falling below the national average.

These differences highlight the economic and social disparities between economically disadvantaged (poor) census tracts and the average census tract across the United States. These census tracts qualify for special consideration regarding community development opportunities, not due to the concentration of households of a particular race, but because of these household economic statistics.

Instead of riding off into the sunset, HBCUs can leverage their prominence in these census tracts to spearhead community and economic development initiatives. The disparities between these census tracts' economic and demographic data and the average U.S. census tract highlight numerous community and economic development opportunities.

HBCUs can leverage these differences for positive change by implementing economic revitalization strategies that consider the lower income levels and higher poverty rates in many of these census tracts. Targeted investments in these areas can stimulate local economies, create jobs, and improve living standards. Supporting local entrepreneurs and small businesses can foster economic growth and cultivate a more vibrant community.

Investing in education and job training programs can help residents acquire the skills necessary for better employment opportunities. Enhancing access to healthcare services can improve overall community health and productivity. Developing affordable housing can address low homeownership rates and enhance living conditions. Upgrading infrastructure, such as transportation and public facilities, can improve quality of life and attract further investment.

Initiatives that engage residents in decision-making processes can empower communities and ensure that development projects meet their needs. Supporting cultural and social programs can strengthen community bonds and promote a sense of pride and identity. Advocating policies that address systemic inequities can create a more level playing field and ensure that development benefits all residents.

Enhancing access to credit and financial services empowers residents to invest in their futures and accumulate wealth. Emphasizing these aspects, community and economic development initiatives can foster sustainable and inclusive growth, positively impacting the census tracts and society as a whole. Below are examples of successful case studies in community and economic development within majority Black census tracts:

North St. Louis, Missouri

For many years, North St. Louis has struggled with ongoing poverty, population decline, and lack of investment. The region is marked by elevated poverty levels and notable racial disparities. Initiatives have been launched to assist local businesses and contractors to foster economic development. This involves enhancing schools and facilities in community centers to bolster neighborhoods. The aim is to combine advanced manufacturing with inclusive growth to generate employment opportunities.

Harlem Children's Zone, New York

Harlem, a historically Black neighborhood in New York City, has struggled with high poverty rates and poor educational outcomes. The Harlem Children's Zone provides services that include early childhood education and college support. These programs aim to involve the entire community, including parents and local organizations, focusing on enhancing academic results through charter schools and after-school initiatives.

East Lake, Atlanta, Georgia

East Lake was once characterized by high crime rates and low-income levels. Significant challenges persist in redeveloping public housing into mixed-income communities. The establishment of a charter school and health facilities aims to support residents. Additionally, partnerships with local organizations and residents are essential to ensure sustainable development.

These case studies illustrate how targeted investments, community involvement, and extensive support can foster vibrant community and economic development in the census tracts where HBCUs are situated.

CHAPTER 5

The Principal Mission

5.1 Building Community

The HBCU designation was granted to higher education institutions established before 1964, whose "principal mission" was the education of Black Americans. To fulfill this mission, HBCUs had to undertake tasks that encompassed more than simply addressing the educational needs of the communities they served.

In the beginning, achieving the "principal mission" meant teaching the foundations of education to Black Americans who were routinely and deliberately denied even the most rudimentary literacy training. The denial of educational opportunities was the primary tool that allowed chattel slavery to be practiced for so long in America.

Education equipped individuals with the skills to navigate an escape and create documents that would disprove any claims of ownership upon fleeing. The ability to read and write formed the foundation of what it meant to be free in America.

After slavery was abolished and these institutions began to fulfill their mission of educating the Black community, the tasks necessary for achieving this mission started to transform into those required to establish a free Black community. The people of African descent were involuntarily brought to the American colonies and deliberately deprived of any knowledge of their cultural heritage, which held the elements they needed to create a stable Black community.

This forced separation from the knowledge of their ancestors placed them at a significant disadvantage in functioning as a cohesive community. Therefore, as its "principal mission," the HBCU educational network had to teach its students how to piece together the remnants of their shared African origin to form a Black community and culture.

Therefore, from the beginning, achieving the HBCU's "principal mission" included providing a nurturing environment that emphasized education and offered people of African descent a refuge within the United States while acquiring the knowledge needed to secure their freedom. The principal mission was never just about teaching the previously enslaved how to read and write but also about sharing the cultural knowledge necessary to thrive and survive as a Black community in America.

HBCUs and their surrounding communities became known as places of safety, comfort, and pride for these previously enslaved people. The remnants of African culture played a significant role in the development and survival of the community, and HBCUs became repositories of this cultural knowledge, serving as the foundation of the Black community.

By achieving their primary mission, HBCUs became the focal point of the Black community in the Southern and Northern states, a source of the community's stability and economic success. By the beginning of the twentieth century, the HBCU educational network had successfully improved the financial status of the Black community by providing it with the knowledge necessary to compete in the free market economy.

Starting at the most basic level, the foundations of the HBCU educational curriculum evolved to encompass the key principles and elements that form the basis for effective teaching and learning. The HBCU educational network gradually evolved to meet the growing demand for knowledge, a top priority for the Black community.

The mission started with reading, writing, and mathematical skills necessary for further learning and daily life. Then, it expanded to effective verbal and written communication, including listening, speaking, and writing, which is crucial for academic and professional success.

The education included teaching the ability to analyze, evaluate, and synthesize information to make informed decisions and solve problems. This led to a basic understanding of scientific principles and the ability to apply scientific methods to explore and comprehend the natural world.

Understanding and appreciating diverse cultures, histories, and perspectives that foster empathy and social cohesion was included. Developing self-awareness, self-management, social awareness, relationship-building, and responsible decision-making skills was essential to the curriculum.

An education on how to use and understand technology, which is essential in the modern world, was included. Equally important is understanding and applying ethical principles and values, such as honesty, integrity, and respect for others.

The curriculum promoted physical health and well-being through regular exercise and knowledge of healthy lifestyle choices. It also encouraged creative thinking, artistic expression, and the ability to innovate and adapt to new challenges.

These foundational elements provide a comprehensive framework for the HBCU educational network, helping the Black community develop the skills and knowledge necessary to thrive in their personal, academic, and professional lives. The emergence and transformation of the Black labor force by the HBCU educational network is one of the great success stories of the Industrial Revolution in the United States.

The success of the first wave of HBCUs established immediately after the Civil War was followed by a second, more significant wave, aided by graduates of the first wave, the wealth generated during the Gilded Age, and the second Morrill Act of 1890. The illiterate Black labor force that existed at the end of the Civil War transformed into a labor force capable of competing successfully in the emerging industrial economy.

The early HBCU business model, which transitioned the Black community into the free labor market, required a curriculum that included vocational training, teacher education, and liberal arts and sciences. This curriculum met the immediate needs of the Black community by fostering direct student participation in building the campus and the surrounding community.

These curriculum elements, combined with the funding sources, created a sustainable business model that allowed HBCUs to fulfill their mission of providing quality education to Black students despite significant financial challenges and social opposition. Early HBCUs relied heavily on funding from religious organizations, philanthropic foundations, and donated campus sites. While tuition and fees were a source of revenue, many HBCUs maintained low tuition to remain accessible to students from diverse family incomes and backgrounds.

The Black community's involvement, including donations and volunteer labor efforts, was crucial for their sustainability, and the HBCU alums played an especially vital role in this business model. HBCU alumni supported the development of the HBCU educational network through donations and fundraising efforts, and they served as advocates, administrators, faculty, and staff of these institutions.

The Freedmen's Bureau provided the first source of federal funding during Reconstruction by confiscating land to use as campus sites. Another example of federal funding was the Morrill Acts, which eventually required state governments to include HBCUs as recipients of federal land-grant programs. These programs established colleges by providing financing in the form of federal land grants to be sold, raising money to construct the campus.

The Higher Education Act of 1965 was a game-changer for every institution of higher education in the United States. It strengthened the educational resources of all colleges and universities, providing financial assistance to students in postsecondary and higher education. This Act played a pivotal role in enhancing the capacity and sustainability of HBCUs, ensuring they could continue to provide quality education to their historically underserved communities.

One of the primary legacy effects of this Act was Title III, which increased federal funding for HBCUs and provided support to enhance their academic resources and facilities. Title III of the Act included provisions to strengthen developing institutions by providing a direct federal budget, which helped improve their infrastructure, educational programs, and student services.

The Act increased access to higher education for Black students through programs like Pell Grants and Upward Bound. These programs provided financial support to low-income students, enabling more Black students to attend college, and were crucial for the survival and growth of the historically underfunded HBCUs.

Over the years, amendments to the Higher Education Act have continued to provide targeted support for HBCUs. For example, the 2008 reauthorization included the HBCU Capital Financing Program, a loan program that helped schools improve their physical infrastructure.

This federal assistance was much needed and overdue because educating the Black community was prohibited by long-held discriminatory beliefs and constructed legal and illegal means to impede the development of the HBCU educational network by the white political power structure.

Still, the HBCUs' "principal mission" has not changed, and data support the premise that HBCUs may be better equipped to achieve this mission than PWIs. When Black students are in the minority of a student body, they must confront long-standing racial biases and stereotypes.

Even if PWIs are not purposefully negligent, their history of discriminatory practices forces Black students to deal with cultural demands that take away from their focus on studying and opportunities for self-discovery that the college experience should provide. In contrast, HBCUs offer a supportive and inclusive environment where Black students can thrive academically and socially without facing the subtle and overt forms of discrimination often present in PWIs.

They foster a strong community among Black students, faculty, and staff, promoting unity, solidarity, and empowerment. They also offer opportunities for Black students to learn from and be mentored by successful Black professionals, inspiring them to achieve their full potential. HBCU alumni networks offer valuable connections and support, enabling graduates to advance their careers and contribute to their communities.

HBCUs have a long history of producing influential leaders in various fields, including politics, business, engineering, medicine, education, and the arts. HBCU curricula often incorporate courses that delve into Black history and cultural contributions, and maintain historical sites, museums, and archives that document the experiences and achievements of Black people.

Black cultural initiatives and events are hosted and launched on HBCU campuses, alongside homecoming celebrations, Greek life activities, artistic performances, and celebrations of Black culture and traditions. HBCUs empower Black students to succeed academically and personally, while contributing to developing and preserving Black history, culture, and community.

Today, to complete the "principal mission," HBCUs must compete with PWIs, which are achieving a significant degree of success in attracting and educating Black students. Along with improvements to PWI campuses funded by the Higher Education Act of 1965, Title VI of the Civil Rights Act of 1964 explicitly prohibited PWI from discriminating based on race, color, or national origin in programs and activities receiving federal financial assistance, thereby protecting Black students' right to attend the college of their choice.

Attracted by more extensive course offerings, modern campus infrastructure, and convenient residential, retail, and commercial availability, Black students took advantage of the opportunity to attend PWIs. The survival of the HBCU educational network depends on how well HBCU administrations respond to this competition.

The preservation of HBCUs accomplishes two critical objectives: eliminating racial discrimination in American life and preserving Black history and culture as a valuable contribution to modern civilization. To continue this work, HBCUs must augment their business models to obtain the investments required to attract and maintain student enrollment and transform their campuses and communities into destination places that continue to attract quality students, faculty, and staff.

This investment is necessary to improve the infrastructure of the institution and the surrounding communities, which have always nurtured and supported the students, faculty, and staff. Without this investment, HBCUs cannot play their crucial role and utilize their key advantages in performing the tasks required to complete their "principal mission."

Today, the primary tasks essential for fulfilling the principal mission of educating the Black community include restoring the Black community surrounding the HBCUs, preserving Black history and culture, and continuing efforts to remove racial discrimination from American democracy. Educating the Black community necessitates a comprehensive understanding of its past, an accurate evaluation of its present condition, and a strategic plan for its future.

This knowledge is essential for the Black community to understand itself as it continually struggles to create a place for itself in the world. Continuing to meet this "principal mission" requires these institutions to expand beyond the traditional contributions of church missionaries, founder philanthropists, and government funding to include private sector investment in and around HBCU campuses.

The HBCU educational network provided essential opportunities that were denied to people of African descent, and consequently, it developed a loyal following among Black people. The communities and families, fortunate enough to be part of these institutions, are part of a treasured legacy that has built the Black community and will remain supporters and participants in any new HBCU venture.

The HBCU educational network must continue to provide a nurturing environment for the students, faculty, staff, and supporters who reside within its gates and extend into the surrounding communities. HBCUs' business model should be updated to ensure that the HBCU educational network and the Black community survive in this age and the next.

The "principal mission" of HBCUs always will be to perform and complete the tasks required to transform the campuses and surrounding communities that comprise the HBCU educational network into a Beloved Community for the Black community and America.

The concept of the Beloved Community represents a beautiful vision of a society rooted in justice, equal opportunity, and a genuine love for all humanity. This inspiring idea was popularized by Dr. Martin Luther King Jr., who viewed it as the ultimate goal of the Civil Rights Movement. In the Beloved Community, we find a warm and welcoming spirit of friendship and goodwill, where all forms of discrimination, poverty, and violence are no longer present.

Dr. King articulated the concept of the Beloved Community as a societal vision in which conflicts are addressed through peaceful means and justice triumphs. He posited that nonviolence is the fundamental approach to realizing this community, underscoring the importance of love and understanding as catalysts for converting adversaries into allies. King's speeches and writings consistently underscore this vision, aspiring toward a world in which brotherhood and sisterhood manifest as a tangible reality within all dimensions of social existence.

HBCUs have played a crucial role in fostering the Beloved Community by providing education and opportunities to African Americans. These institutions have nurtured leaders who advocate for social justice and equality. HBCUs emphasize community support and the development of the whole person, aligning with the principles of the Beloved Community. They create environments where students can thrive academically and socially, preparing them to contribute positively to society.

The Civil Rights Movement was fundamentally anchored in the ideals of the Beloved Community. Activists aimed to establish a society devoid of racial segregation and discrimination, allowing all individuals to exist with dignity and respect. Inspired by Dr. King, the movement emphasized a nonviolent approach to bring about social change through love and peaceful resistance. The Beloved Community's vision offered a moral compass that directed the efforts and aspirations of civil rights leaders.

5.2 The HBCU Golden Age

On the eve of the Civil War in 1860, the U.S. government lacked a clear plan of action for the 4 million enslaved Black people in the country. However, the war's dynamics and the daily actions of the opposing armies enabled the enslaved individuals to develop their own strategies. The plan of the enslaved Black people was to leverage the war as an opportunity to secure their freedom.

Northern industrialists supported a plan that favored free labor, while the Southern planters, whose cotton production dominated the world economy, aimed to maintain slavery indefinitely. The plans of the moral abolitionists included rewriting the Constitution, which did not adequately condemn slavery. However, that plan was highly unlikely because their moral opposition did not outweigh the economic and political benefits of slavery.

The plans of the four candidates for the 1860 presidential election concurred on the legality of slavery in the United States. They acknowledged that its practice was protected under the laws of the Constitution. However, they differed on whether slavery should be allowed to expand into every state and compete with free labor.

Abraham Lincoln, of the Republican Party, opposed the expansion of slavery into the western territories but did not call for immediate abolition in the states where it already existed. His position focused on preventing the spread of slavery and promoting free labor. Stephen A. Douglas of the Northern Democratic Party advocated "popular sovereignty," which meant that the decision to allow or prohibit slavery in a territory should be made by the settlers rather than by the federal government. John C. Breckinridge, representing the Southern Democratic Party, advocated for the protection of slavery in the territories and the states' rights to decide on the issue of slavery. He believed in the expansion of slavery and its protection under the Constitution. John Bell of the Constitutional Union Party sought to avoid the issue of slavery altogether, focusing instead on preserving the Union and upholding the Constitution. His stance aimed to appeal to moderate voters in both the North and the South.

After President Lincoln's victory, these irreconcilable differences led to a civil war between the states in less than six months. The war prompted the opposing armies to develop a strategy that involved utilizing the enslaved Black people as a resource to assist them in their efforts to win the conflict.

Although the opposing armies reacted similarly, more enslaved people were attracted to the Union Army because they did not recognize the enslavers' right to ownership and were willing to compensate the enslaved for their labor and contributions toward winning the war for the Northern states.

The church and missionary organizations that opposed the practice of slavery and traveled to the front lines of the war to support the Union Army aided the enslaved who fled during the conflict. The actions of these groups acted as a catalyst for implementing a plan of action for enslaved people, which would endure after the war's conclusion.

The enslaved people's plan of action led to the establishment of contraband camps where enslaved runaways could secure their freedom, food, clothing, and shelter while supporting the Union war effort. This plan resulted in the creation of contraband camp schools, which evolved into the HBCU educational network, facilitating the transition from slave labor to free labor and laying the groundwork for the development of the Black community. Following the war's end, several pieces of federal legislation (the Reconstruction Acts and Amendments) to protect formerly enslaved individuals in the southern states were added to the plan.

Although no official name or recognition of a specific action plan existed, the dynamic forces of the Civil War added new chapters to the evolving plan of action. The efforts of the Northern Army evolved into the Freedmen's Bureau, which was officially authorized to support and protect the HBCU educational network and foster the development of the Black community.

Missionary organizations, such as the American Missionary Association (AMA) and the American Home Mission Society (AHMS), which supported the Union Army's war effort, collaborated with the Freedmen's Bureau. With contributions from Northern philanthropists, they established several HBCUs to support the postwar action plan. The graduates of these institutions were quickly sent to staff new public schools to help develop more HBCUs.

These graduates became the leaders of a network of HBCUs, which included multiple institutions in every southern state. For all practical purposes, establishing the HBCU educational network and the surrounding communities became the official action plan for the 4 million Black Americans who gained freedom during and after the Civil War. The HBCUs are the only remaining evidence that a plan of action existed.

Initially, donations from church missionary organizations and Northern philanthropy primarily funded the HBCU educational network. The Morrill Act of 1890 provided indirect federal and state funding to increase the development of HBCUs because the act required Southern states that practiced racial discrimination to establish state-funded HBCUs for every state college funded by the Morrill Act that did not allow Black students to enroll.

During the Great Depression, the HBCU educational network and the surrounding Black communities benefited from the limited economic options available to the Black community in the Northern states. These campuses attracted residential, retail, and commercial development, as local migrants were no longer drawn to Northern jobs during this period. HBCU communities became primary destinations for the Black community, on a scale equal to or exceeding that of the Black church and local public schools, which were also key centers of the Black community.

At this point, the HBCUs are the story's protagonists for transitioning the people from illiteracy to literacy, from slavery to free labor, from involuntary servitude to citizenship. The services provided by the HBCU educational network have created a generation dedicated to advancing and uplifting the Black race, symbolizing a deep commitment to racial pride, social justice, and the fight against racial oppression.

HBCU graduates in the labor force are leaders in their communities, advocating for civil rights, education, and economic opportunities for the Black community. They embody and promote a sense of pride in Black heritage and culture, countering the negative stereotypes and systemic racism prevalent in society. Their work often involves significant community service aimed at improving the living conditions and prospects of the Black community.

According to the book *Black Bourgeoisie: The Rise of a New Middle Class in the United States* by E. Franklin Frazier, HBCUs' educational network was recognized as the most influential component of the Black community after World War II, and its graduates were at the forefront of the growing Black middle class. In addition, HBCU graduates were leading the way and achieving genuine political and social change against racial discrimination in the United States and worldwide.

This is the point in most famous stories (Anakin Skywalker/Darth Vader in *Star Wars*, Walter White in *Breaking Bad*, Light Yagami in *Death Note*, Macbeth in *Macbeth*, Harvey Dent/Two-Face in *Batman*, Michael Corleone in *The Godfather*) where the protagonist undergoes a transformation and becomes the antagonist. Often, the catalyst for this transformation is the protagonist's overwhelming success and unexpected challenges to the new position of power.

No significant changes occurred in the HBCU education network until Title VI of the Civil Rights Act of 1964 and the Higher Education Act of 1965 were passed as part of the Great Society legislative program. The Higher Education Act of 1965 provided substantial federal aid, providing an unprecedented amount of the college-age population to enroll into college. Title VI caused a shift in enrollment patterns by prohibiting PWIs from refusing to enroll Black students, thereby encouraging Black students to enroll in PWIs.

Maintaining enrollment growth is essential for the success of higher education institutions. These institutions usually incur significant fixed costs, such as buildings, administrative staff, and faculty expenses, which remain constant even during a decline in enrollment. To alleviate the negative effects of these substantial fixed costs, higher education institutions need stable and consistent enrollment growth.

This change in the dynamics of the enrollment pattern for the Black college-age population is the dilemma that transformed the HBCU protagonist into the antagonist. To ensure financial success, HBCUs' leadership must proactively address this shift in enrollment patterns and implement strategies to promote enrollment growth. Title VI of the Civil Rights Act of 1964 posed a significant threat that prompted HBCU leadership to adapt to changing enrollment patterns as Black students opted to attend PWIs instead of HBCUs. The adjustments made to respond to these evolving enrollment conditions can turn an HBCU from a protagonist into an antagonist.

To determine how an HBCU is impacted, this book contains historical and demographic data for all HBCUs, compiled to create a model of the economic structure of a typical HBCU. This enables an analysis of the impact of changing market conditions on the financial framework of HBCUs and provides a method for developing appropriate adjustments to the HBCU business model.

This technique enables testing various strategies to determine which modifications to the typical HBCU business model yield the best results. It also facilitates creating a customized business strategy for a specific HBCU, leveraging its financial and demographic data.

The data used to develop this technique reflect the daily activities of over hundred HBCUs and their communities. This information outlines the financial infrastructure of the HBCU educational network as it has evolved since its inception.

These data indirectly include the components of the HBCU educational network, such as public schools, community organizations, and business and government entities that support the operation of the HBCU community. As a result, adjustments to the HBCU business model create a ripple effect throughout the surrounding community, as reflected in the model.

The data summarize the latest financial and demographic information for over hundred HBCUs mandated to report their data to the U.S. Department of Education and provides a profile of a typical HBCU. Based on this information, HBCUs are, on average, the largest employers and the primary economic engine in their census tracts.

A census tract is a small area within a county designed to represent a permanent statistical subdivision of the county and a homogeneous community regarding population characteristics, economic status, and living conditions. These tracts are uniquely numbered within each county and are used by the U.S. Census Bureau to collect and analyze data to classify each tract based on economic performance.

Census tracts remain stable over time, allowing for statistical comparisons among different tracts. Their boundaries typically follow visible and identifiable features such as roads, rivers, or other geographic markers and range in size from 1,200 to 4,000 inhabitants.

The census tract data collected for the HBCUs indicate that a typical HBCU census tract has an average population of about 2,000 people, with 20 percent of households living below the U.S. poverty level, household income below the state's average, and an unemployment rate above the U.S. average.

Table 5.1 data show that 93 percent of the HBCUs are in census tracts characterized as economically disadvantaged or poor, and 84 percent are located in the old Confederate states. Sixty-four percent are situated in urban communities with populations exceeding 50,000, and 100percent are found in predominantly Black neighborhoods.

However, the model indicates that the continuous influx of Black college students into these communities, the financial assets of the HBCUs, and the infrastructure resources of the surrounding communities have the potential to create a strong engine for economic growth. With appropriate planning and coordination with these communities, it is possible to leverage these resources to attract both private and public financing for the long-term economic development of HBCU communities.

HBCU-led community development can raise typical HBCU enrollment to or above the average for all HBCUs, as shown in Table 5.1, and enhance the economic conditions of the HBCU census tract to or above the statistical average for the census tract in that county. These statistical outcomes apply to many PWIs, which serve as the backbone of college towns that often evolve into hubs of economic opportunity.

Colleges and universities typically drive economic growth in their communities by spending on local goods and services and employing local workers. They also increase the supply of skilled workers by educating potential employees and raise the demand for skilled workers through research and development activities.

The higher education sector tends to contribute stability to a region because it is less susceptible to economic downturns than other sectors. Studies have shown that for every dollar budgeted for higher education, there is a significant multiplier effect on the local economy. These institutions are critical drivers of social, technological, and economic innovation, which makes them valuable assets to their regional economies.

Table 5.1 displays the aggregated level of resources the HBCU educational network has assembled over the years to fulfill the "principal mission" of educating Black Americans. Numerous resources are available to execute and complete the constantly evolving tasks required to achieve the mission, which remains unfinished.

However, these institutions will encounter unique challenges in overcoming the obstacles posed by PWI competition. For instance, the table illustrates that the total endowment of all HBCUs is $4.2 billion, whereas Harvard University alone has an endowment of $40 billion.

The disparity in endowment values highlights the significant funding gap between HBCUs and non-HBCUs, summarizing the only advantage that PWIs have in the competition for Black student enrollment. Their endowment advantage is one that HBCUs will never match, given PWIs' substantial head start in collecting endowments. This head start also impacts their ability to provide financial aid, maintain facilities, support extracurricular activities, and uphold academic programs.

TABLE 5.1 HBCU financial and demographic statistics

Number of HBCUs	105
Privately funded	50%
Publicly funded	50%
Total HBCU endowment	$4,222,544,379
Total HBCU enrollment	283,355
Total HBCU campus acreage	23,669
Total HBCU staff + graduate assistants	58,144
Average HBCU annual revenues	$105,888,342
Average HBCU annual expenditures	$97,997,687
Average population of HBCU locations	256,803
Average HBCU enrollment	2,830
Average HBCU in-state tuition	$16,407
Average HBCU out-of-state tuition	$20,120
Black population 18–24	4,160,359
Black population 18–24 attending college	1,539,333
Percentage of Black population 18–24 attending HBCUs	18%
Percentage of HBCUs located in the southern states	81%
Percentage of HBCUs located in poor census tracts	93%
Percentage of HBCUs located in communities with populations ≤ 100,000	44%
Percentage Black population of HBCU locations	49%
Percentage of HBCUs located in urban areas	64%
Percentage of HBCUs located in rural areas	36%

Source: Department of Education, National Center for Education Statistics (2022), U.S. Census Bureau, and World Population Review (2024).

Therefore, to compete—which HBCUs must do—strategic adjustments need to be made to the HBCU business model to better utilize the resources available to them. The data indicate that the financial foundation and structure of the HBCU educational network are solid; thus, now is the time to evaluate what adjustments to the business model are necessary to mitigate the negative effects of PWI competition and identify the most effective and efficient methods for implementing these adjustments.

5.3 HBCU Business Analysis

Like all higher education institutions, HBCUs are designed to operate indefinitely, possessing all the rights granted to a legal corporate entity licensed by the state. Their services generate numerous direct and indirect economic benefits for society and civilization, which is why governments grant these institutions nonprofit corporation status for tax purposes, similar to religious institutions.

The lifespan of these institutions depends on their ability to maintain accreditation with their regulatory authority, generate total revenue exceeding total expenditures, and maintain adequate financial operating reserves. Therefore, like all corporations, higher education institutions must function based on a business model that generates profit.

The institution's business model is key to determining the length of its hypothetical indefinite lifespan. It provides a clear framework for aligning all business elements to achieve the institution's goals and generate profit. A business model is a strategic plan that outlines how an institution creates, delivers, and captures value. Its core aspects include target customers, value proposition, revenue streams, cost structure, and key activities.

Higher education institutions initially adopted a straightforward business model that relies on the commitment of founders, students, and alumni to generate a revenue stream sufficient to cover the expenses of meeting the community's higher educational needs. However, as the community's demands grew, the business model of higher education institutions evolved to secure the financial resources necessary to drive the economic growth needed to support expanding community needs beyond education.

The business models became more complex and evolved to create research that developed business and economic mobility engines needed to address the community's expanding needs. This was not the evolutionary path of an HBCU's business model due to limitations created by the HBCU's principal mission. HBCUs were designed exclusively to address the educational needs of the Black community.

The HBCU business model could not be expanded to meet the economic demands of the Black community because the legal practice of racial discrimination in the Southern states restricted HBCUs' access to the financial resources required to enhance the economic capacity of the Black community. Racial discrimination limited the ability of HBCUs and surrounding communities to benefit from the economic growth generated by the more complex business models of non-HBCU higher education institutions. The missionaries designed the basic HBCU curriculum to confer Bachelor of Arts degrees rather than to produce the research that led to business development. Students demonstrating those skills were encouraged to attend PWIs to obtain advanced degrees.

The early HBCU business model, developed by the missionary founders of these institutions, relied heavily on in-kind services provided by its target customers, the formerly enslaved students, to operate, maintain, and build the campus facilities. The curriculum's goals included vocational training, teacher education, liberal arts, and sciences, which equipped students with the immediate skills needed to support the HBCU and the surrounding community.

This business model was designed to work under the segregated social structure established by Southern state governments that restricted the free flow of trade and commerce between the white and Black races. The curriculum elements, combined with funding from donations by religious organizations, philanthropic foundations, tuition and fees, and financial support from the Black community, were a sustainable business model that allowed HBCUs to offer quality education to Black students despite significant economic and social challenges

The applicability of the HBCU business model was severely challenged after the passage of Title III of the Higher Education Act of 1965. Title III provided funding directly to college students, allowing them to attend any college without requiring in-kind services as a condition of enrollment. Today's students are far more likely to receive government-backed student loans, grants, or scholarships, or pay for tuition, fees, and room and board with income provided by their families.

In addition, Title VI of the Civil Rights Act of 1964 enforced the right of Black students to attend college, live in communities outside the HBCU educational network, and pursue careers beyond the curriculum offered at HBCUs. Title VI enforced the laws against discrimination by denying federal funding to institutions that practiced discrimination due to race, sex, or religion, opening previously closed windows of opportunity for Black students.

Finally, HBCU student involvement in the Civil Rights Movement decreased funding from many of their traditional religious and philanthropic contributors, whose financial support for HBCUs declined after watching HBCU students engage in actions of civil disobedience. These changes to the educational marketplace significantly impact the effectiveness of the traditional HBCU business model, which established privately and publicly funded HBCUs. Therefore, HBCUs' business models require a serious update.

Publicly financed HBCUs are entitled to state funding equal to the per-student amount allocated to white-only institutions under the Morrill Act of 1890 provisions. However, the Southern state governments seldom allocated HBCUs funding equal to that of the white-only public institutions created using the Morrill Act due to the practice of racial discrimination, except after legal deliberations and court orders.

A recent strategy to change the HBCU business model is to press the states for an equitable share of state funding in response to what appear to be Morrill Act violations. The strategy suggests that HBCUs should receive funding equal to that obtained by white-only institutions over the years under the Morrill Act requirement. This strategy, known as "the states must pay," has merit and works occasionally and is described in the book, *The State Must Provide: Why America's Colleges Have Always Been Unequal—and How to Set Them Right*, by Adam Harris. Still, state legislatures are reluctant to fund HBCUs in equal proportions to white-only institutions, especially since these white-only institutions are no longer white-only. The admittance of Black students to what once were white-only institutions raises questions among state legislators regarding the continued need for state funding for HBCUs.

The HBCU business model needs to be adjusted to address these changes in the educational marketplace. The main impact of these marketplace changes is the loss of traditional HBCU revenue streams due to the opportunity and the decision of Black students to enroll in PWIs and decreased contributions from the institution's founding contributors.

Another critical component of the HBCU business model that needs updating is expanding the model to include the HBCUs' economic impact on the surrounding communities. The laws that opened the doors of white-only higher education institutions also removed financial restrictions placed on investing in HBCU communities. They enforced the opportunity to access economic resources, allowing HBCUs to include community needs and development in the HBCU business model.

The principal mission of HBCUs, defined as educating the Black community, limited the services they could provide due to business and social restrictions that accompanied the practice of racial discrimination. Non-HBCU higher educational institutions did not face the same limitations, and their business model included projects that expanded the economic growth of their surrounding communities.

Consequently, non-HBCUs developed their surrounding communities to attract students, faculty, staff, and businesses to the institutions. These communities and institutions work with industry and government to convert their campuses into research centers representing the nation's most prosperous commercial centers and residential neighborhoods.

For example, some of the most successful university-based research centers in the United States are Harvard University (1636) and Massachusetts Institute of Technology (1861) in Cambridge, Massachusetts; Stanford University (1891) in Palo Alto, California; University of California (1868) in Berkeley, California, University of Texas (1883) in Austin, Texas, University of Michigan (1817) in Ann Arbor, Michigan, University of Illinois (1868) in Champaign, Illinois, University of Wisconsin (1848) in Madison, Wisconsin (1848), and Georgia Institute of Technology

(1885), in Atlanta, Georgia, none of which are located in economically disadvantaged census tracts.

The communities surrounding these universities are known for their strong entrepreneurial ecosystems, which foster innovation and collaboration between academia and industry. They have significantly contributed to economic growth and the nation's technological advancement. Adjusting the HBCU business model to achieve this level of success does not require a new government mandate or program. It starts with the HBCU leadership authorizing an evaluation of the HBCU business process needed to update the business model.

5.3.1 EVALUATION

The institutional evaluation includes a document analysis, a process analysis, and an impact analysis. The evaluation's purpose is to quantitatively and qualitatively measure how the institution is performing its mission as envisioned by its official leadership body and how effectively it is achieving the goals as outlined by the leadership. Another key purpose of the evaluation is to determine whether the institution's organizational structure has adequate infrastructure in place to assess what is achieved from the appropriation of its resources.

Document analysis involves reviewing all documents, whether paper or online, used to collect or distribute institutional information. The purpose of this analysis is to assess what information is being collected regarding the institution's activities and is available for examination, as well as to identify what additional information needs to be gathered for a comprehensive evaluation.

The process analysis compares the institution's procedural documents to the actual practices of the institution's staff in performing the required day-to-day activities. This analysis assists in determining if the procedures are being followed and which institutional practices need adjusting to ensure the institution uses its resources effectively and efficiently.

The impact analysis compares the estimated output of the institution's annual budget to the institution's actual output. This analysis reveals what the institution receives for its resources and the return on the institutional investment in funded activities.

These three analyses work together in an iterative process that provides insight into how the business model should be revised to generate the desired output and achieve the "principal mission." The mission is to develop an environment that excels in the education of Black Americans, builds a prosperous Black community, preserves Black culture, and fosters the democratic principles envisioned by the Beloved Community.

5.3.2 BUSINESS MODEL ANALYSIS

Once the institutional evaluation is completed, the business model components are calculated from the data collected, which includes:

Total Revenue: This includes all the institution's income, such as tuition fees, investment income, government funding, donations, grants, and auxiliary services (e.g., housing, dining).

Total Cost: This encompasses all expenses incurred by the institution, including educational expenses, salaries, administrative costs, maintenance, utilities, and other operational expenses.

Average Fixed Cost (AFC): These costs do not change with the output level (e.g., permanent staff salaries, building, and maintenance). AFC is calculated by dividing total fixed costs by the number of students.

Average Variable Cost (AVC): These costs vary with the level of output (e.g., materials, part-time staff wages, enrollment). AVC is calculated by dividing total variable costs by the number of students.

Average Total Cost (ATC): These are the total costs incurred by the institution, calculated by dividing Total Cost by the number of students, or cost per student.

Price: This is the tuition fee charged to students. It can vary based on factors such as in-state versus out-of-state status, program of study, and additional costs.

Quantity: This refers to the number of students enrolled at the institution.

Break-Even Point: This is the point at which total revenue equals total costs, meaning the institution is not making a profit but also not incurring a loss. It is calculated by dividing total fixed costs by the difference between the price per student and the average variable cost per student.

Price–Average Total Cost: This relationship determines if the institution's tuition collected from each student does not, does, or is equal to the annual cost the institution incurs to provide the student with an education.

These analytical tools help determine which adjustments the HBCU business model requires to compensate for the educational market changes adversely impacting their ability to stay in operation. The model allows for different outcomes by varying the value of its components.

In most cases, the data used to perform this analysis are available from the data used to develop the institution's annual balance sheet, profit and loss statement, and financial audit. If an institution has difficulty producing these documents and the documents that validated these data for the last three years, then this HBCU requires an update to its business model.

Let us assume the following annual financial information needed to develop a business model can be obtained for an HBCU:

- Total fixed costs: $10,000,000
- Total variable costs: $5,000,000
- Total cost: $15,000,000
- Number of students: 1,000
- Tuition fee per student: $20,000

Once collected, these financial data can be used to calculate the business model components that need to be adjusted to achieve the desired business performance.

Average fixed cost (AFC) = Total fixed costs / Number of students = $10,000,000 / 1,000 = $10,000

Average variable cost (AVC) = Total variable costs / Number of students = $5,000,000 / 1,000 = $5,000

Average total cost (ATC) = Total costs / Number of students = \$15,000,000 / 1,000 = \$15,000

After the average cost calculations are completed, the model can perform two tests that provide the insight needed to achieve the HBCU's desired mission: the break-even point test and the price–average total cost test.

Break-even point (BEP) = Total fixed costs / (Price – AVC) = \$10,000,000 / (\$20,000 – \$5,000) = 667 students

The calculation means the institution must enroll at least 667 students to cover the institution's fixed costs, but more insight is available. Using actual HBCU data to calculate the break-even point provides the following significant insights into the financial condition of the HBCU:

Financial Health: This helps determine whether the institution can cover fixed and variable costs with its current revenue. The institution consistently operating above the break-even point indicates financial stability.

Cost Management: By analyzing the break-even point, institutions can identify areas to reduce costs or improve efficiency. This can lead to better financial management and resource allocation.

Revenue Strategies: Understanding the break-even point can help institutions develop strategies to increase revenue, such as adjusting tuition fees, increasing enrollment, or seeking additional funding sources.

Decision Making: It provides a basis for making informed decisions about investments, expansions, or cutbacks. Knowing the break-even point helps administrators understand the financial implications of their choices.

Risk Assessment: It allows institutions to assess the financial risks associated with enrollment, funding, or expense changes. This can help in planning for contingencies and ensuring long-term sustainability.

The break-even point is a valuable tool for assessing financial conditions and making strategic decisions for the future of an institution of higher education.

Price–average total cost = \$20,000 – \$15,000 = \$5,000

This means the institution is collecting more tuition from students than the cost to the institution, but more insight is available. Calculating the difference between price and average total cost (ATC) can provide significant insights into the financial condition of an HBCU or any institution of higher education.

Profitability: If the price (tuition and fees) exceeds the ATC, the institution is generating a profit for each student. Conversely, if the price is lower than the ATC, the institution is operating at a loss.

Cost Efficiency: Analyzing the ATC helps institutions identify areas to reduce costs or improve efficiency. This can lead to better financial management and resource allocation.

Pricing Strategy: Understanding the relationship between price and ATC can help institutions develop effective pricing strategies. For example, they can adjust tuition fees to cover costs while remaining competitive.

Financial Planning: This calculation aids financial planning and budgeting by clearly showing the institution's cost structure and revenue generation.

Sustainability: It helps assess the institution's long-term sustainability. Consistently operating with a price above the ATC indicates financial health, while the opposite suggests potential financial challenges.

These calculations are valuable tools for assessing financial conditions and making informed decisions for the future of an institution of higher education.

Only after these data and documents are available can a cash flow analysis and an estimate of permanent working capital for the HBCU be carried out. Performing a cash flow analysis and estimating permanent working capital can significantly benefit HBCUs.

5.3.3 CASH FLOW ANALYSIS

A cash flow analysis can help HBCUs ensure they have sufficient cash to meet short-term obligations such as payroll, utilities, and other operational expenses. It can also aid in forecasting future cash flows, enabling improved budgeting and financial planning.

A cash flow analysis can aid decision making by providing insights into areas where costs can be reduced or revenue can be increased. This decision-making process offers potential investors and donors a clear understanding of the institution's financial health and stability, which can attract more funding. It helps identify potential financial problems early, allowing for timely corrective actions.

Cash flow analysis is a vital financial tool that assists businesses and individuals in understanding their cash inflows and outflows from various activities over a specific period. Cash inflows from operating activities include revenue from enrollment, services, and other operations.

Cash outflows refer to expenses such as salaries, rent, utilities, and materials. Cash inflows from investing activities include the sale of assets, dividends, and interest earned. Cash outflows also encompass the purchase of assets, investments in securities, and loans given. Cash inflows from financing activities encompass loans and other financing activities, and cash outflows consist of loan repayments.

The purpose of cash flow analysis is to manage liquidity by ensuring the institution has sufficient cash to meet its short-term obligations and to provide insights into areas where costs can be reduced or revenues increased. This information is critical for financial planning, which forecasts future cash flow and budgets, offering potential investors a view of the institutional financial health and stability. The analysis of the institutional financial structure is essential for developing the long-term private financial commitment needed to enhance campus and community infrastructure improvements.

5.3.4 PERMANENT WORKING CAPITAL

Evaluating permanent working capital ensures operational stability for HBCUs by estimating and maintaining a minimum level of cash and current assets to support day-to-day operations, thereby reducing the risk of financial disruptions. It establishes a foundation for long-term financial planning and sustainability, assisting HBCUs in preparing for future enrollment growth and campus development.

It is part of the efficient allocation of resources, ensuring that funds are available for essential activities and projects, which enhances the overall financial health of the institution by maintaining a balance between current assets and liabilities. By performing these analyses, HBCUs can better manage their finances, plan effectively, and ensure their continued resiliency in providing quality education and support to their students.

Estimating permanent working capital involves analyzing the company's historical financial data and understanding its operational needs. The process includes identifying the institution's core current assets, such as readily available funds for day-to-day operations, money owed to the institution, often from tuition, fees, and grants, short-term investments that can be quickly converted to cash, supplies and materials used in the institution's operations, prepaid expenses, accounts receivable, and cash reserves, which are necessary for daily operations.

Analyzing historical data involves reviewing past financial statements to identify the average levels of these core current assets during a semester or school year. The review focuses on the minimum levels of current assets, excluding any temporary increases due to seasonal demand or short-term projects. Calculate the average of these minimum levels to estimate the permanent working capital. Permanent Working Capital refers to the minimum level of current assets the institution must maintain to ensure smooth operations during the semesters and summer seasons. It represents the ongoing investment needed to support day-to-day activities during the financial cycle of an academic year.

Updating the HBCU business model is mandatory for any HBCU that still relies on the business model used by the original missionary and philanthropy founders. There is merit in maintaining the continuity represented by the original administration building, which was financed by the efforts of the founders during the Industrial Revolution era. However, there is no merit in using the same strategic planning structure instead of the Information Revolution era analytics used in 21st-century strategic planning techniques.

CHAPTER 6

This Is How We Do It

6.1 Start with a Plan

The abolitionists, missionaries, and Army officers who served as the first HBCU administrators required minimal planning to attract the initial students, faculty, administrators, and residents to the HBCU communities established to transition the formerly enslaved Black population into their well-deserved freedom. The establishment of the initial HBCU communities benefited from a combination of incentives that created an overwhelming desire within the first participants: the promise of freedom from ownership upon arrival, an opportunity to address the social problems caused by slavery, the chance to acquire the knowledge needed to thrive in a free market economy and a chance to start a meaningful and gratifying career in education.

However, more planning and coordination were necessary, as the success of the first HBCUs reinforced their desire to establish an educational network capable of disseminating the knowledge required for enduring freedom throughout the Southern states. These HBCU founders devised plans that leveraged their close connections to missionary organizations and Northern businesses interested in restoring cotton production to its prewar level.

The missionaries' connections to Southern churches aided in locating support for the expansion of the HBCU educational network. Many Southerners, including enslavers, were part of these missionary organizations before and after the Civil War. Furthermore, these organizations excelled at raising the funds necessary to finance the construction of HBCU campuses and to recruit and pay faculty and staff.

Their planning benefited from the efforts of post-Civil War Southern state governments, which recognized that public education, including higher, secondary, and primary levels, was a valuable tool for aiding the recovery of the Southern economy. This plan expanded the HBCU educational network and would have continued to grow the network until HBCU students' opposition to racial discrimination gained widespread attention in the 1960s and evolved into the Civil Rights Movement.

The plan encountered opposition due to conflicting views between the HBCU administrators, the original missionary and philanthropic foundations that funded HBCUs, and the student body concerning how and when to end the legal practice of racial discrimination in the South. The former had developed a position that tolerated and accepted racial discrimination in exchange for campus safety, while the latter wanted the practice to end everywhere immediately.

The conflict changed the parameters of the HBCU educational network and altered the plan's effectiveness for its future growth. HBCU presidents could no longer adhere to the hundred-year-old plan used to expand the HBCU education network after their students' involvement in the Civil Rights Movement.

The passage of Great Society legislation in the 1960s primarily resulted from plans initiated by nonviolent HBCU student revolutionaries to raise public awareness and generate support among the American people for the Civil Rights Movement. This support enabled Congress to pass laws aimed at ending racial discrimination and providing relief for its victims. The dynamics of the decision-making process for the Black college-age population and the Black community drastically transformed following the enactment of this legislation.

The passage expanded options for members of the Black college-age population in determining which educational environment offers the best learning experience. The legislation included financial assistance to attend college regardless of family household income and the choice to enroll in any PWI that had previously denied Black students the right to enroll solely based on race.

The successful passage of this legislation resulted in a significantly higher percentage of the Black college-age population choosing to attend college, increasing from 5 percent before to 36 percent after the passage. Increased college enrollment and the elimination of racial employment practices positively impacted the economic opportunities available to the Black community, further driving the demand for college attendance among Black college-age individuals.

The passage of the legislation ended HBCUs' monopoly on where the Black college-age population would attend college. Before the enactment of the legislation, 90 percent of Black college students attended HBCUs, while today, only 10 percent do. However, this outcome was inevitable, as HBCUs lacked the capacity to accommodate the increased enrollment among the Black college-age population that chose to take advantage of the educational opportunities provided by the Great Society legislation.

And despite what on the surface appeared to be PWIs' permanent opposition to Black student enrollment, the change in the dynamics of choice facing the Black college-age population benefited PWIs that enrolled Black college students. The financial benefits of this boost to enrollment growth and the potential loss of federal funding overpowered discrimination-based objections to Black student enrollment.

Higher education institutions' business models include a higher percentage of their costs as fixed costs than most business entities. One of the most cost-effective steps an institution can take to offset the impact of high fixed costs is to increase enrollment. So, the PWIs no longer objected to enrolling Black students and now aggressively pursued their enrollment.

The implementation of the Great Society legislation altered the dynamics of the choice process for the Black population, changing the fate of HBCUs and the choices available to the Black community. As Black college students chose not to attend HBCUs exclusively, residents of the Black community also decided to take the better jobs and fair housing opportunities provided by the legislation and not to reside solely in the Black community.

The Equal Employment Opportunity Act and the Fair Housing Act of the Great Society legislation significantly impacted the national economy and the Black community. These acts increased Black household income by providing access to higher-paying jobs and improved housing opportunities by ending discriminatory practices in the labor and housing markets.

Discrimination artificially caps market prices, which increase once the practice of racial discrimination is eliminated from the marketplace. Discrimination allows markets to develop dual pricing structures based on racial preference instead of merit, adversely impacting the operation of a free competitive market and diminishing its benefits.

The nonviolent HBCU student revolutionaries' recommendations for inclusion in the Great Society legislation of the 1960s were to end racial discrimination, provide economic assistance to its victims, develop the Black community, and enhance Black and American culture. However, these student revolutionaries, like most revolutionaries, had no plans for what to do if their proposals for change were, in fact, successful.

This legislation, which is still in place, can still be used to change the dynamics of the development of HBCUs, the Black community, and its culture. The initial implementation of this legislation had some unplanned impact on the Black community because no plan was made for what to do if the plans of the nonviolent HBCU student revolutionaries worked.

Now, it is time to fashion a plan to use this legislation and build on the success of the nonviolent HBCU student revolutionaries. A plan that uses this legislation to impact the choice process of the remaining 64 percent of the Black college-age population who have yet to participate in obtaining the knowledge needed for freedom.

Now is the time for the HBCU leadership to develop a plan in their boardroom to use this legislation developed on their campuses to improve the HBCU community. A plan to attract a portion of the remaining 64 percent of the Black college-age population to HBCU dorm rooms and a more significant portion of the Black population back to HBCUs and the surrounding communities.

6.2 Strategic Planning Process

Planning is tricky because it requires a belief in the capacity to accurately predict the future while also recognizing the inability to predict the future accurately. However, one should not be discouraged by the need to plan. Since accurately predicting the future is unlikely, a plan relies on the most accurate available information regarding the current conditions and imagines how changing certain aspects could lead to better future outcomes. This planning process is known as strategic planning.

Strategic planning originated from military strategy, which involved maneuvering forces into advantageous positions before engagement. Ancient texts like Sun Tzu's "The Art of War" provide early examples of strategic principles. The term "strategy" comes from the Greek word "strategos," meaning "general of the army." Greek strategoi offered strategic advice on managing battles to win wars.

The business sector later adopted it to enhance organizational efficiency and competitiveness, and Harvard Business School developed one of the earliest strategic planning methodologies for private businesses in the early 1920s. This strategic planning model defines strategy as a pattern of purposes and policies that guide a company, focusing on managing risk, industry growth, and market share.

Corporate leaders widely embraced strategic planning to enhance competitiveness. This practice distinguishes the thought process from action and establishes a new function staffed by specialists: strategic planners. Strategic planners boost competitiveness by evaluating the outcomes of proposed budgetary goals before implementation, comparing proposed performance against actual performance, and formulating recommendations for improvement.

Over the years, strategic planning has adapted to data analytics and data-driven decision making, including environmental scanning, SWOT analysis, and stakeholder engagement. Environmental scanning involves an internal assessment of the institution's strengths, weaknesses, resources, and capabilities, as well as an external evaluation of opportunities and threats in the environment, encompassing economic, social, technological, and political factors.

Strengths, weaknesses, opportunities, and threats (SWOT) analysis helps organizations navigate complex markets. It is instrumental in setting business goals and objectives, evaluating the efficiency and effectiveness of budget allocation, and developing resilient and sustainable responses to market changes. It continues to be a vital tool for achieving long-term success.

Stakeholder engagement involves faculty, staff, students, alums, and community members planning to gather diverse perspectives and ensure buy-in. Data regarding each group's outlook on the institution are collected and included in the strategic planning process.

In the 1980s and 1990s, higher education institutions began to adopt strategic planning to respond to changes in enrollment patterns that created competition among the institutions for students. Adding the changing characteristics of the college-age population to the list of considerations for the institution administrators required a more rigorous approach to planning.

Strategic planning was aligned with the technological advancements adopted on most institutional campuses, which were employed to collect and analyze data from various operational processes. It also facilitates the incorporation of internal fiscal changes and external demands.

Strategic planning is a comprehensive process that involves several key steps to enhance an institution's long-term success and alignment with its mission and goals. First and foremost, the strategic planning process must be seamlessly and officially integrated into the institution's leadership bylaws and policies to develop its annual budget.

Integrating the strategic planning process with the budgeting process ensures the involvement and, ultimately, the support of every institutional member in the strategic planning process. Effective strategic planning engages every organization member and enables everyone to comprehend their role in achieving the institution's mission and vision. When adequately executed, every staff member understands and can articulate their contribution to the institution's strategic plan.

The institution's leadership requires and approves the strategic planning process; the work that goes into building the strategic plan starts with each member defining their contribution to the institution's mission. The institution president coordinates with each academic department, administrative office, and auxiliary of the institution to develop a multiyear strategic plan linked to an annual budget reviewed by a committee of the board of trustees before final approval by the board.

6.3 Strategic Plan Components

The following items represent an outline of the components of the strategic planning process. However, the most crucial function of the strategic plan process is to show the relationship between the institution's long-term goals and multiyear objectives and how these multiyear targets are aligned with annual performance measures and the operating budget.

1. Establish a mission and vision statement to define the institution's purpose, core values, and goals for the future. HBCUs established this long before the Higher Education Act of 1965 described it as their "principal mission." The principal mission of the HBCU is to educate and build the Black community and preserve Black culture.
2. Establish specific, measurable, achievable, relevant, and time-bound (SMART) goals and objectives that align with the institution's mission and vision. Goals set an organization's overarching direction and vision. Objectives break down these goals into specific, actionable steps. Outcome measures are the tangible results of achieving these objectives. Performance Measures are used to track progress and determine the success of the objectives and goals. Organizations can ensure a cohesive and effective strategic planning process that drives continuous improvement and success by aligning goals, objectives, outcomes, and performance measures.
3. Establish strategies to achieve identified goals and objectives. This may include academic programs, research initiatives, community engagement, and resource allocation. Strategies define the actions and plans needed to achieve goals and objectives.

4. Establish budgets that allocate the necessary financial resources to support the implementation of the strategies. Performance measures track and evaluate the effectiveness of strategies to attain the desired outcomes. Aligning strategies, budgets, and performance measures can ensure a cohesive and practical approach to achieving goals and objectives.

This is an example of how this alignment helps optimize resource allocation, improve decision making, and drive continuous improvement.

- Goal—Improve student retention rates at a university.
- Objective—Increase first-year student retention rates by 10 percent over the next academic year.
- Strategy—Implementing a mentoring program to increase first-year student retention.
- Budget—Allocating a specific amount to fund a first-year student mentoring program.
- Outcome Measure—Percentage improvement of first-year student retention rates.
- Output Measure—Number of first-year students retained.
- Explanatory Measure—Number of first-year students enrolled.
- Explanatory Measure—Number of first-year students participating in the mentoring program.

5. Establish a detailed action plan outlining the steps, timelines, responsibilities, and resources needed to implement the strategies. Ensure the financial, human, and physical resources are allocated effectively to support the strategic initiatives. Execute the action plans, involving coordination and collaboration across various departments and units within the institution.
6. Monitor the progress toward the goals and objectives using the performance measures. Evaluate the effectiveness of the strategies and adjust as needed to stay on track.
7. Inform stakeholders about the strategic plan, progress, and any changes. Effective communication ensures transparency and maintains engagement.
8. Review the strategic plan to ensure it remains relevant and responsive to changing circumstances. This may involve revising goals, strategies, and action plans as needed.

Strategic planning is an ongoing, dynamic process that helps higher education institutions navigate challenges, seize opportunities, and achieve their long-term vision.

6.4 Asset-Based Community Development

Community development is a process where community members come together to take collective action and generate solutions to common problems. It involves building strong and resilient communities by enhancing the skills, knowledge, and confidence of individuals and groups within the community. The goal is to create positive changes by addressing the social, economic, and environmental issues that affect the community.

Community development has roots that stretch back centuries, but as a formalized approach, it took shape in the mid-twentieth century. In the United States, the concept gained significant momentum during the 1960s and 1970s with the War on Poverty and the establishment of community action agencies through the Economic Opportunity Act of 1964.

This legislation, which aimed to combat poverty by promoting self-sufficiency and empowering local communities, was not a tool that the HBCUs were inclined to use, as the hundred-year-old HBCU business model was based on maintaining a dichotomy between their campus and the surrounding Black community. This dichotomy was best described in Ralph Ellison's *Invisible Man*, which won the National Book Award for Fiction in 1953, making Ellison the first Black American author to win this award.

The book contrasted the orderliness and civility of the HBCU campus with the absence of both in the surrounding community. This was so pronounced that the hero of the book, an HBCU student, was expelled from the college when he inadvertently led a visiting white founder on an unscheduled tour of the community surrounding the HBCU campus.

Was art imitating life, or does life imitate art? Nevertheless, HBCUs' unique circumstances regarding their surrounding communities require a distinct approach to community development. The dilemma involves building a cohesive community out of one community that is an active institution of higher education and another economically disadvantaged community, while preserving the distinctive characteristics of the census tract in which both communities are located.

The HBCU solution requires a community development strategy that does not involve tearing everything down and starting from scratch. This strategy must provide HBCU students with services comparable to, or even better than, those offered in the community surrounding a PWI campus while preserving the culture of the area's historical residence.

Asset-Based Community Development (ABCD) is a sustainable, community-driven development strategy that leverages a community's strengths and assets. This approach, developed by John Kretzmann and John McKnight founders of the Asset-Based Community Development Institute, presents a divergent path to community development because it begins with a clear commitment to discovering a community's capacities and assets instead of starting the process by focusing on its needs, deficiencies, and problems.

The ABCD process allows the HBCU to increase the perceived valuation of the census tract by leading the process that begins by calculating the community's value, which can serve as an asset to leverage additional financial resources. This process involves several steps for asset valuation, starting with identifying the community's abilities and expertise. It necessitates high community involvement and establishing tangible community relationships that encourage residents to act sustainably.

The ABCD process starts with asset mapping, which involves developing an inventory of the community's assets. This begins with the individual skills and talents of the community members, recognizing the value of their abilities and expertise. The inventory includes local institutions, such as schools, churches, businesses, and other organizations that can contribute to community development, as well as community physical resources, such as buildings, land, and infrastructure, that can be utilized for community projects. Cultural assets may include traditions, stories, and cultural practices that enrich the community.

The ABCD process allows the HBCU to initiate community engagement, which is the most critical component in determining the valuation of community assets. It actively involves community members in the development process to ensure their voices are heard and their contributions are valued. This includes collaborative planning, in which the community develops a shared vision and plan for its future by conducting listening sessions to gather input from community members through meetings, surveys, and interviews.

The ABCD approach allows the HBCU to reinforce its community relationships by strengthening connections among community members and organizations to foster collaboration. Mutual support is essential to adding value to the community's assets. This involves building networks that create opportunities for community members to connect and share resources. These networks lead to partnerships and alliances with local organizations, businesses, and government agencies.

Mobilizing assets means using the identified community assets as leverage to attract additional financial resources to address community challenges and achieve development goals. This is part of the ABCD project implementation, which develops and executes projects by leveraging community assets. This implementation process ensures that resource allocation occurs effectively to support community initiatives.

HBCUs require sustainable development based on long-term solutions that build on the community's strengths and promote self-reliance, which is at the core of the ABCD strategy. ABCD involves capacity building by providing training and support to enhance community members' skills and capabilities. It also includes evaluation and adaptation, which means continuously assessing the impact of development efforts and adjusting as needed.

ABCD provides benefits that improve community development results by emphasizing the importance of local knowledge and resources. It empowers communities to drive their development and create lasting positive change. This environment enhances HBCUs' efforts to address the challenge of revising their century-old business model.

ABCD empowers communities to take control of their development, fostering a sense of ownership and responsibility. By building existing assets, ABCD creates solutions that are more likely to be sustainable in the long term. ABCD encourages the participation of all community members, ensuring that diverse voices are heard and valued. By strengthening local connections and building existing resources, the ABCD approach can help HBCUs bridge gaps with their surrounding communities and become more resilient. In summary, Asset-Based Community Development is a powerful approach to community development that allows HBCUs to focus on strengths rather than weaknesses and empowers their surrounding communities to drive positive change.

6.5 Alumni Support

In his book, *The Education of Black People*, W. E. B. Du Bois argues in support of HBCUs for various reasons. The most compelling is summarized in the following statement:

> Our history in America, north, south, and Caribbean, has been an extraordinary one, which we must know to understand ourselves and our world. The experience through which our ancestors have gone for four hundred years is part of our bone and sinew whether we know it or not. The methods which we evolved for opposing slavery and fighting prejudice are not to be forgotten but learned for our own and others' instruction….Many Negroes do not realize this. In their haste to become Americans, their desire not to be peculiar or segregated in mind or body, they try to escape their cultural heritage and the body of experience which they themselves have built-up. This is the reason that there is always a certain risk in taking a colored student from his native environment and transplanting him suddenly to a Northern school. He may, through the help of his own social group in the neighborhood of this school, successfully achieve an education through the facilities offered. On the other hand, he may meet peculiar frustration and in the end be unable to achieve success in the new environment or fit into the old.

According to Du Bois, the HBCU setting creates the best cultural environment for Black students aspiring to learn the life lessons needed to survive under the various circumstances presented to them in the Americas. Preserving this cultural experience requires that the institution's funding not be left up to the states or the gifts of the rich.

In his opinion, HBCU graduates should take responsibility for providing 100 percent of the financial resources needed to fund these schools as insurance against mission drift. Moreover, HBCUs should design their curriculum so that their students recognize the importance of such financial commitment and ensure they fulfill it upon graduation.

The unique circumstances that led to the creation of HBCUs stemmed from the struggle of families representing the African people who were forced into involuntary servitude in the Americas. More importantly, it reflects the struggle for American democracy to realize its true potential.

For this reason and others, HBCUs should make a genuine effort to ensure that their graduates are provided ample opportunities to give back to the institution in a way that makes a difference in its outcome. While responsibility for 100 percent of the institution's funding may be considered an extreme ask, there should be a reasonable target that every HBCU can realistically strive to meet.

Figures 6.1 and 6.2 visually summarize the primary sources of public and private college funding in 2025 and their estimated share of the total budget.

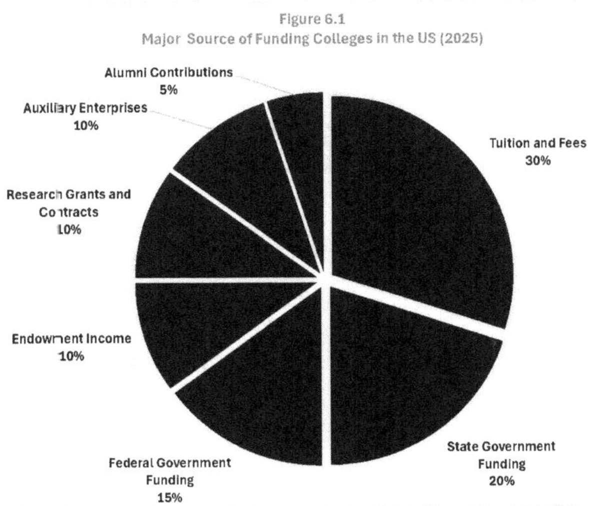

FIGURE 6.1 Major source of funding colleges in the United States (2025)

As a rule, alumni giving is not measured by the percentage of the institution's budget funded by alumni contributions. Typically, alumni contributions represent less than 5 percent of the institution's budget. Therefore, alumni giving is measured annually as a percentage of alumni contributing to the institution. The average alumni giving rate for the 2022–2023 academic year was 7.7 percent, based on data from 282 ranked National Universities and National Liberal Arts Colleges in an annual U.S. News survey. Notably, some institutions reported significantly higher figures, with the top 20 colleges achieving an impressive one-year average alumni giving rates of nearly 27 percent.

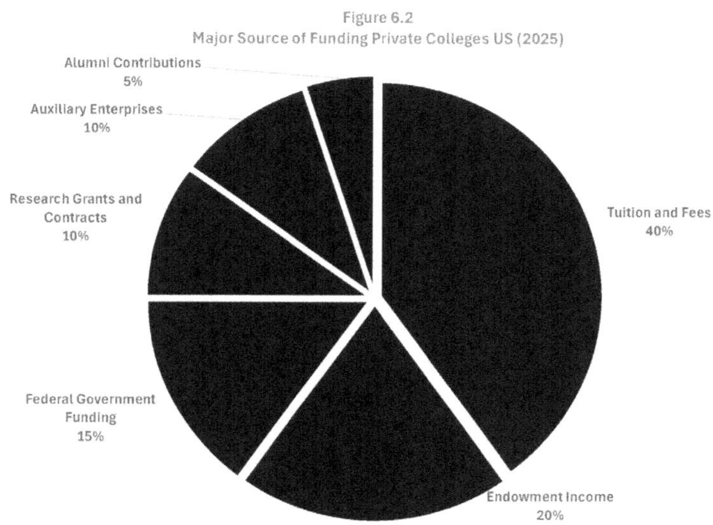

FIGURE 6.2 Major source of funding private colleges in the United States (2025)

Among the twenty colleges, Princeton University in New Jersey reported the highest average alumni giving rate for the 2022–2023 academic year at 46.6 percent. In contrast, Yale University in Connecticut, another Ivy League school, had the lowest rate at 19.7 percent. Of the top 20 institutions, only two—Southern Illinois University—Carbondale and the U.S. Military Academy at West Point in New York—are not private. Additionally, three women's colleges are in Massachusetts: Mount Holyoke, Smith, and Wellesley.

Hampton University in Virginia stands out as the only HBCU on this list, which might represent a target for HBCUs in setting a goal for alumni giving that is not unreasonable. Based on these data, a reasonable HBCU dual goal for alumni contributions might be an alumni giving rate of 25 percent and an annual share of the budget of 5 percent.

Generating alum support involves a strategic approach that focuses on building strong relationships, engaging alumni, and demonstrating the impact of their contributions. Creating this support should be a top priority for HBCUs and worthy of a place in the annual budget. Generating alumni support is a process composed of several activities that, when executed together, form a substantial and resilient level of alumni support.

It begins with creating an alumni database that maintains an up-to-date and comprehensive record, including contact information, career details, and engagement history. The database should be expandable and compatible with the latest technology industry standards. The data needed to build the database should be available, as it is the institution's ongoing responsibility to maintain official transcripts on student enrollment.

While protecting privacy, the database must implement an effective multichannel outreach and communication strategy to keep alumni informed and engaged, including newsletters, social media, emails, and personal outreach. The plan highlights success stories, institutional achievements, and opportunities for involvement.

Moreover, fostering sustained alumni support necessitates offering engagement opportunities, such as reunions, networking sessions, and webinars, to cultivate a sense of community and connection among alumni. Provide volunteer opportunities, such as mentoring current students, serving on advisory boards, or participating in fundraising campaigns.

Recognition and appreciation strengthen alumni commitment. This is achieved by acknowledging and celebrating alumni contributions through awards, recognition events, and public acknowledgments in institutional publications. Personalized thank-you messages and updates on the impact of their support are vital to this process.

Fundraising campaigns should target and align with alumni interests and passions, such as scholarships, research initiatives, or campus improvements. Incorporating matching gift programs, crowdfunding platforms, and planned giving options is essential to maximize contributions. Offer exclusive benefits in return for support, such as access to campus facilities, discounts on continuing education programs, and career services.

Collect data from every event to enable a data-driven approach. Utilize data analytics to identify trends, segment alumni based on their interests and engagement levels, and tailor outreach efforts accordingly. Monitor and evaluate the effectiveness of alumni engagement strategies, adjusting as needed. Employ storytelling to share compelling stories that illustrate the impact of alumni support on the institution and its students. Highlight alumni's personal and professional achievements to inspire pride and connection.

Collaborate with academic departments to identify and engage alumni strongly connected to specific programs or disciplines. Involve faculty in outreach and engagement efforts with alumni. Focus on building long-term relationships that begin while they are students and continue throughout their lives. Create a culture of giving and engagement that is deeply rooted in the institution's values and practices.

HBCUs are equipped with the tools required to implement these strategies and can cultivate strong alumni support, enhance financial stability, and foster a vibrant, engaged alumni community. What is required is setting the goals, identifying and assigning the resources to implement the plan, and working the plan until the goal is reached.

6.6 Campus Master Planning

The campus master plan (CMP) is a transformative tool that can profoundly impact students' higher education experiences. It guides the creation of a physical environment that immediately changes a student's life upon stepping onto the campus, delivering an inspiring and unique educational experience that aligns with the college's academic mission.

The CMP is a steadfast commitment to institutional sustainability and establishes the physical guidelines necessary to maintain the effectiveness and efficiency of the learning environment over time. It is a cornerstone of the college's long-term success and instills a sense of reassurance and confidence in its future.

The CMP creates the space required to support students' transformative educational journeys when enrolling in college. It fosters a clear campus identity that reinforces a sense of community among students, faculty, staff, administration, and the surrounding campus.

The day-to-day demands of running a higher education institution compel its leadership to allocate substantial time to short-term operational decisions. However, parallel to these demands, the institution must engage in long-range planning to ensure that its mission effectively coordinates competing goals related to academics, research, student life, athletics, outreach, service, and support programs. The CMP guides this long-range implementation, ensuring the effective coordination of the institution's day-to-day actions and mission.

The CMP fulfills the long-term mission and vision outlined in the institution's strategic plan. This plan articulates the institution's most comprehensive vision of itself as an educational entity and details how it will allocate its financial and other resources to achieve those goals.

The CMP translates the long-range plans of the strategic plan into a physical campus master plan that designates the locations of buildings, open spaces, circulation systems, utilities, and other elements of the campus environment. The CMP serves as the vehicle that provides institutions with the resilience and capacity to withstand or quickly recover from unforeseen difficulties, which challenges the stability of the campus's learning environment.

6.6.1 CAMPUS MASTER PLAN—BEST PRACTICES

The CMP can be presented in various formats that employ different planning approaches. However, the best practices in CMP design include at least the following:

- Institutional Mission and Strategic Plan
  The college must achieve its mission, vision, objectives, and goals outlined in the strategic plan, including measurable targets for academic and enrollment outcomes.

- The Campus Controller Planning Process
  Developing the CMP must include summary input from the college administrative leadership, staff, faculty, students, and community stakeholders.

- Background Analysis
  Building a foundation for the CMP requires an assessment of the institution's history, the campus' existing conditions, and its capacity to fulfill its academic commitment to the students.

- Planning Framework
  Planning for the CMP is guided by the mission, strategic plan, and academic focus, which must be reflected in the space occupied by the college and used as the learning environment for the students. The planning framework must also address the issues identified during the background analysis.

- Campus Master Plan Elements
  To prepare the CMP properly, it is essential to include land use and site design, academic facilities, open space, housing, circulation, public facilities, and infrastructure. In addition, the CMP should consist of building and landscape design guidelines and extend to the surrounding community.

- Safety and Security
  Maintaining campus safety and security must be embedded in the CMP and involves input and coordination with the campus police and local and regional public safety and emergency response agencies. The campus safety and security features should accommodate the fluctuating number of people on campus daily and the campus's ability to attract many people from off campus.

- Implementation Strategy
  Implementing the CMP involves outlining strategies that include priority setting and phasing that can obtain funding for improvements over five to ten years. Im-

plementation requires more detailed planning, capital construction, operational changes, and ensuring continuity in decision making. Ongoing project monitoring and updating can occur regularly. Most importantly, CMP needs to blend the long-term capital cost into the short-term operational needs of the campus.

- Adoption and Approval
  Adopting the CMP requires approval from an internal Steering Committee before being submitted to the governing body for final approval. As the ultimate decision-making authority, the governing body reviews the CMP to ensure it aligns with the institution's mission, vision, and strategic plan before giving the final approval to implement the CMP.

- Formats and Audiences
  The CMP includes a traditional booklet that can be downloaded for reference. Additionally, it comprises an executive summary and other concise versions for broader dissemination, along with the comprehensive plan.

The institution must have the facilities—including buildings, open spaces, circulation systems, and utility infrastructure—to effectively serve its students, faculty, staff, and guests. Creating a well-designed educational space that is functional, aesthetically pleasing, safe, sustainable, and supportive of the college's academic mission is essential.

The CMP presents a comprehensive vision for the desired educational space, accompanied by an implementation program to reach this objective. CMPs are also utilized for various internal and external purposes:

- Marketing to increase enrollment
- Analyzing potential for future physical development
- Guiding building and landscape design
- Supporting capital campaigns and improved funding opportunities
- Creating and enhancing corporate partnerships
- Improving community and campus relationships
- Increasing operating efficiencies
- Improving space allocation and utilization
- Attaining board approvals

Good CMPs are adaptable and responsive to changes in program needs. Many institutions use a regular review to gauge progress and adjust to accommodate programmatic changes. Intervals of two to five years are usually adequate to recognize changes in academic programs, technology, and other needs that will drive adjustments to the plan. During these reviews, the CMP is evaluated against the institution's current needs and goals, and adjustments are made to ensure it remains relevant and practical.

It is essential to reexamine the CMP's premises and principles occasionally. The most common circumstances in which a significant new planning process should be initiated include the following:

- A change in leadership
- A revision of the institution's strategic plan
- A significant change that affects the physical development of the campus
- A modification of the academic program mix
- A change in pedagogy
- An increase in students residing on campus
- A technological breakthrough
- A focus on environmental sustainability
- A significant, anticipated increase in enrollment
- An opportunity to expand campus lands nearby or at a different site
- New regulatory requirements or funding opportunities

6.6.2 CAMPUS MASTER PLAN—INNOVATIONS

The CMP for the future campus is no longer limited to a two-dimensional picture. While maps are helpful, they are static and quickly become outdated once completed. Relying solely on a formal map with set beginning and end points is restrictive and makes it difficult to make necessary adjustments. It's time to embrace a more dynamic process that allows flexibility and adaptability.

New CMPs must be viewed as an ongoing, adaptable process that is programmatically driven and integrated with long-term campus plans, notably the strategic plan. In the current climate, universities and colleges must adapt to constant change.

However, this also presents unexpected opportunities. Even in unforeseen situations, the CMP must be able to guide decisions with authority.

The recursive relationship between the strategic plan and the CMP is crucial. The mission directs the strategic plan, while the CMP process informs the administration about issues and opportunities the strategic plan must address. Rapidly changing technology and public awareness of global environmental change provide two excellent examples of the dynamic context of campus planning and how universities must respond to new circumstances and conditions.

Previously, CMPs have always been visually distinctive, with unique grounds and buildings that stand out. The development pattern is vastly different, with larger land parcels, more open space, and massive structures. Additionally, campuses are often identified by boundary walls and gates, specific landscape patterns and vegetation, the utilization of courtyards, and a cohesive architectural style for groups of buildings.

CMPs have significantly developed by moving away from the outdated "ivory tower" model, once deemed the best learning environment. The emphasis now lies on community engagement and leadership. This shift is reflected in how institutions' physical structures are integrated into the community without walls or barriers. Furthermore, with technological advancements, colleges and universities can now be present virtually anywhere.

Moreover, it should be noted that even a college that houses all its students and has sufficient land to accommodate its academic and support needs is not an isolated entity within or adjacent to its municipality. Its utilities must be connected, and services may become intermingled. While colleges and universities maintain their infrastructure within the physical campus, they may collaborate with the community to use shared facilities such as water and sewage treatment plants as capital partners or as bulk consumers. Depending on the size and nature of the institution, they may also engage in mutual aid agreements for public safety, fire protection, and emergency services.

A college or university's spatial influence may extend beyond its campus boundaries. Noncontiguous parcels for educational or related purposes are crucial to campus planning, especially at the community–campus interface. Nearby businesses and services are also vital for students. However, real estate holdings for investment purposes or unrelated uses are only typically included in the CMP if they are being held for future expansion.

Therefore, to revise the hundred-year-old business model, the HBCUs must broaden their focus beyond the traditional definition of the campus itself. They must also consider the possibility of future expansion, the interface between the campus and the surrounding community where a mix of campus-related and noncampus uses occur, and the surrounding district as defined by the city or town where the college or university is situated.

CHAPTER 7

Doing More, Better, Faster

7.1 The Civil Rights Gap

Civil rights are the fundamental rights and freedoms that belong to every person, regardless of race, gender, nationality, religion, or other characteristics. These rights ensure individuals can participate in society's civil, political, and economic life without discrimination or repression.

Civil rights include the freedom of speech, the freedom of assembly, the freedom of religion, the right to privacy, the right to a fair trial, the right to vote, and the right to equality in public places. These rights protect individual freedoms and promote social and economic justice.

They are often enshrined in laws and constitutions to safeguard against government abuses and ensure everyone is treated equally under the rule of law. These rights were not granted to the people of African descent brought to America under the terms of involuntary servitude, creating a civil rights gap between them and their European counterparts.

Over the years, HBCUs have accumulated the assets, technical expertise, and cultural and historical knowledge required to close the civil rights gap between American immigrants of African and European descent. The HBCU's "primary mission" was to provide basic education to the Black community, formed by the people of African descent, and to provide them with the knowledge needed to survive post-enslavement.

This mission evolved into using the acquired knowledge to create a culture that contained survival skills and to obtain fundamental civil rights for the Black community. The distribution of this knowledge led to the successful delivery of these skills and rights, eventually earning the members of the Black community the equality necessary to close the civil rights gap and survive and thrive in a free-market economy.

The success of the Civil Rights Movement closed the civil rights gap by facilitating the passage of the Great Society legislation. It opened up unlimited economic opportunities for the Black community and the U.S. economy. As a result, Black people experienced unprecedented economic growth during the 1960s and a decrease in the violent strategies used to suppress Black economic growth.

However, closing the civil rights gap diminished the role HBCUs and the Black community played in closing the economic gap. The new economic opportunities in jobs and housing led to the abandonment of these institutions, which, ironically, were the source of the new economic opportunities for the Black population.

These institutions served as the economic engines that led to the success of the Black population and their ability to integrate into every sector of the U.S. economy. This outward flow of talented resources led to the economic decline of the traditional Black community and a widening of the Black economic gap.

The HBCUs' success in closing the civil rights gap did not close the gap between the economic performance of the Black community and the rest of the U.S. economy. Although other institutions are now participating in the effort to close this financial gap, there is a unique role that only HBCUs are positioned to perform in this effort.

Because they are in these communities, HBCUs are uniquely positioned to close the Black community's economic gap. The HBCU educational network is positioned to address the legacy of involuntary servitude and promote the remnants of the community's African heritage. The HBCU educational network includes the Black communities surrounding the HBCU's location and is the most acceptable candidate to lead the community's economic development.

The primary cause of the economic gap was the legal practice of racial discrimination, which included overtly violent strategies to suppress the Black communities' efforts to compete in the free market economy. Through the work of HBCU nonviolent student revolutionaries, the legal practice of racial discrimination was removed from the free marketplace to give the Black community a better chance to compete and close the economic gap.

While eliminating legal racial discrimination did help close the civil rights gap, it did not finish the primary mission of these institutions. To close the Black economic gap, these institutions must do more to finish the economic development of the Black community.

The solid knowledge-based foundation of HBCUs provides a platform to do more in economic development, as a universe of options exists under the HBCU umbrella. Only internal organizational or infrastructural limitations impede these institutions from pursuing more aggressive strategies to close the economic gap for their students and the residents of their surrounding communities.

The overt use of violence that was once used to suppress economic activity in the Black community is no longer aided and abetted by the governmental authorities of the jurisdiction where HBCUs are located. The Black community's and the HBCU's assets still form an economic engine capable of stimulating positive economic opportunities within their census tract.

What economic action to pursue depends on the financial and demographic parameters of the HBCU and the surrounding community. However, to close the economic gap, the HBCU must decide to lead the surrounding community in doing more.

The primary mission of HBCUs has not changed over the years, but the tasks they must perform to ensure the Black community is educated have evolved. These tasks have evolved from providing basic literacy to training teachers and preachers to developing a culture, defining a heritage, and acquiring civil rights.

The ability of the HBCU educational network to effectively complete its primary mission is directly related to the economic viability of the Black community. Therefore, to complete the education of the Black community, HBCUs must provide the necessary knowledge and leadership to promote the community and economic development required to close the economic gap.

The probability that the educational efforts of the HBCUs would eliminate the economic gap between those who arrived in America under the terms of voluntary servitude (seven years of enslavement) and those under the terms of involuntary servitude (lifetime enslavement) was undoubtedly low. However, the HBCUs' successful efforts at closing the civil rights gap were the first step in eventually closing the economic gap. The resources needed to close the Black economic gap, like the civil rights gap, are part of the HBCU educational network.

7.2 The Economic Gap

The original intent of the HBCU educational network included a conscious effort to close the civil rights gap and convert once-enslaved Black labor into free Black labor capable of competing in the free marketplace. This was the first step in closing the economic gap created by their enslavement.

It was a coincidence that the skills needed to convert slave labor to free labor were also valuable for encouraging participation and planning the activities that culminated in the Civil Rights Movement, arguably the nation's most influential social uprising, next to the American Revolution. The HBCU nonviolent student revolutionaries who led the struggle for civil rights also advocated for the passage of the Great Society legislation, officially closing the civil rights gap for all Americans.

The legislation that closed the civil rights gap provided access to job and housing opportunities previously denied to Black and underserved communities in the United States. The legislation that removed the civil rights gap also established federal government activities to address the economic gaps existing between all Americans by declaring a War on Poverty as part of the Great Society legislation.

The HBCUs' inspired success in the Civil Rights Movement, which led to the passage of the Great Society legislation, served as an economic stimulus for the U.S. economy. The impact of this stimulus ushered in the beginning of an era of economic prosperity that, for the first time, demonstrated the full potential of the U.S. economy.

This legislation increased the size of the labor force by extending an equal opportunity to participate in the labor force to those previously excluded due to race, color, sex, religion, or other reasons.

The legislation also provided the labor force with additional access to education and technical training, which increased the labor force's quality, productivity, and wage rate.

The increased jobs and wages led to higher incomes, household spending, and gross domestic product (GDP) growth. As a result, the United States stood alone as the leading world economy during the 1960s. The world's industrial economies could compete but were still recovering from the destruction of World War II and were dependent upon production and financial assistance from the United States.

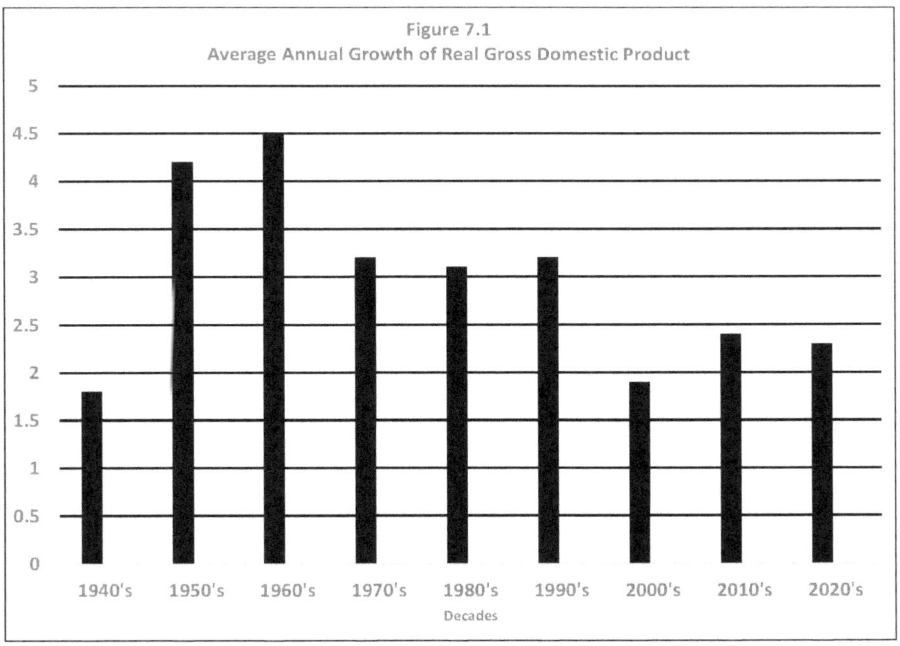

FIGURE 7.1 Average growth of annual gross domestic product

Figure 7.1 shows the 1960s set the standard for economic growth in the United States, as measured by the percentage change in real GDP. During the 1960s, the U.S. economy reached its highest potential growth in real GDP, given the available factors of production.

The impact of the Great Society legislation or any legislation is not immediate. It takes time (recognizing the problem, passing the bill, implementing programs, and measuring the impact) before reaching the people needing the services. Eventually, the legislation's effect reached the people, and the impact could be measured and observed, and to date, the average 5 percent annual growth in real GDP has not been exceeded.

However, the HBCU-inspired success of the 1960s is often overshadowed by the violent rioting that took place in numerous Black communities during that decade. Despite these adverse events, several positive and significant changes reshaped the social and economic structure of the United States during this period.

The first dramatic change was access to job opportunities previously denied due to race, followed by increased income associated with these jobs, a college education that became more affordable due to the additional income, and a decrease in the poverty level, as shown earlier in Figure 4.1 for the Black and U.S. populations.

The 1960s also marked the beginning of the HBCU-inspired expansion in the economic performance of the U.S. Black population, as illustrated in Figures 7.2 and 7.3, which compare unemployment rate and median annual wage rate data for the Black and U.S. populations from 1960 to 2024.

The comparison shows an economic gap between the Black and the U.S. populations, which, on the surface, suggests the need for better economic performance for the Black population. Examining the data is crucial in developing potential recommendations to improve performance.

The unemployment data in Figure 7.2 show a gap between the unemployment rates for the Black population and the U.S. population, which is expected. Over the range of the data, the gap begins to diminish, representing higher employment levels among the Black population.

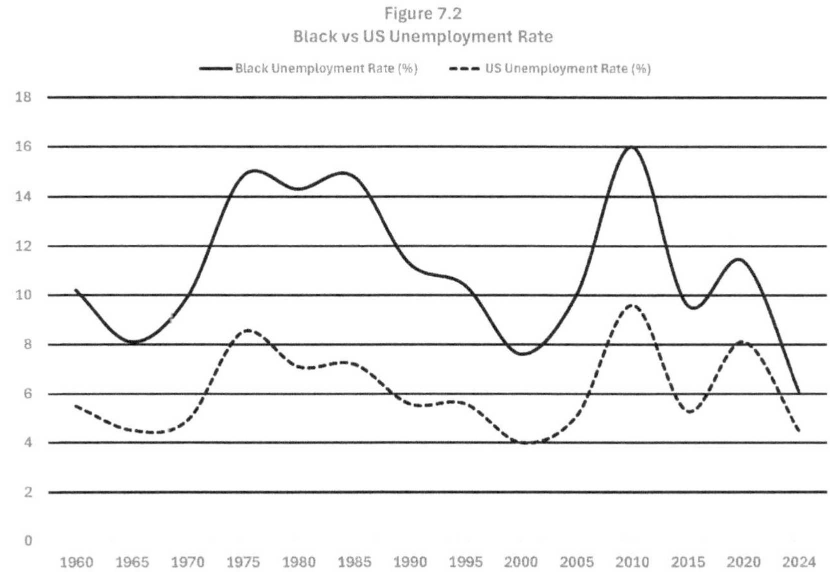

FIGURE 7.2 Black versus U.S. unemployment rate

The expanded availability of job opportunities starting during the 1960s led to the employment of a more significant percentage of the Black population leading up to 2024. While achieving a 0 percent unemployment rate is highly unlikely and undesirable for an advanced industrial economy, having a Black unemployment rate lower than the U.S. unemployment rate is a reasonable goal and achievable by employing a more significant proportion of the Black labor force.

Using the median annual wage rate to measure economic performance, Figure 7.3 shows a ten percent gap between the Black median annual wage rate and that of the United States during the 1960s. This achievement is a vast improvement, given the 100 percent gap that existed one hundred years earlier before the Black enslaved labor force fled their oppressors to find freedom behind the Union Army lines at the start of the Civil War.

However, unlike the unemployment gap, which decreases over time as the Black labor force finds more employment opportunities (Figure 7.2), the wage rate gap is increasing and reaching a high of 44.2 percent in 2024. The Black median annual wage rate increased continually during this period, just not as fast as the wage rate for the United States.

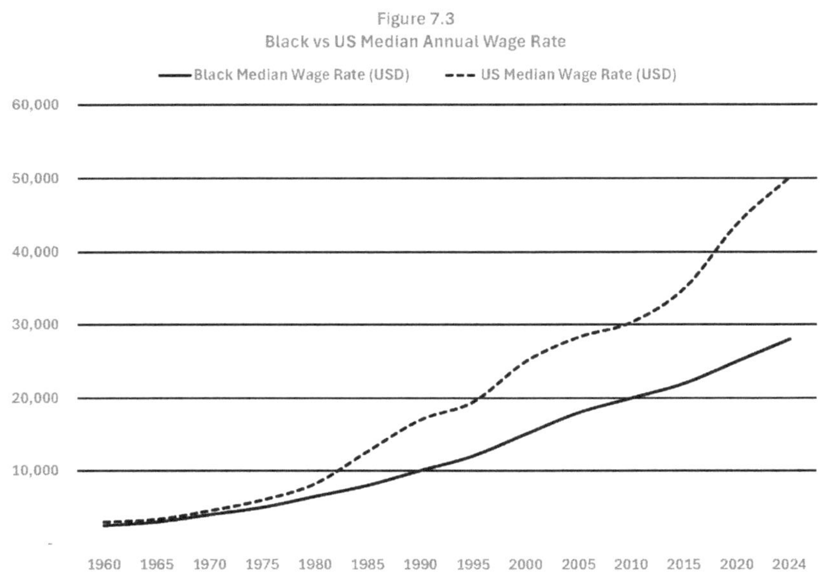

FIGURE 7.3 Black versus U.S. median annual wage rate

From 1960 to 2024, the median annual wage rate increased at an average annual rate of 25 percent and 16 percent for the United States and the Black labor force, respectively.

The unemployment rate and wage rate data demonstrate that the Black labor force received a larger share of the jobs available in the free labor market after the civil rights gap closed during the 1960s, but not necessarily of the highest-paying jobs available.

The data also suggest that to close the economic gap, the Black population needed more than uninhibited access to job opportunities. It must also possess the skills to qualify for the highest-paying jobs in the free marketplace.

Additionally, to augment the increase in wage income, more access to the capital required to increase business and job opportunities within census tracts containing a Black majority population is also necessary to close the economic gap. For example, 95 percent of HBCUs are in census tracts classified as economically disadvantaged (poor), within predominantly Black populations located in the Southern United States.

Now that the civil rights gap is effectively closed, the HBCUs' primary mission of educating the Black population needs to evolve into providing the education required to close the economic gap, just as it evolved from closing a literacy gap to closing a civil rights gap. Closing the economic gap requires providing its students with the skills to qualify for the highest-paying jobs in the free marketplace and the knowledge needed to access the capital necessary to promote business and job growth in the HBCU census tracts and the surrounding communities.

Closing the civil rights gap could not be accomplished until the HBCU education network closed the literacy gap created by the enslavement of the Black population. Likewise, closing the economic gap required closing the civil rights gap, which denied the Black population a competitive opportunity to compete in the free marketplace.

Closing the literacy and civil rights gaps diminished the size of the Black economic gap. A review of the economic data shows that these successes led to an increase in the economic performance of the Black community and unprecedented growth in the U.S. economy.

However, more is required if the HBCU educational network is to succeed at closing the economic gap. The effort and knowledge needed to succeed in this arena will require better performances from the HBCU educational network than it needed to close the first two gaps.

7.3 The Enrollment Gap

HBCUs are the only institutions created in America with the primary mission of educating the Black community. These institutions were established to provide education to a community that had been systematically denied access to education.

Therefore, these institutions are responsible for the condition of the Black community in the United States and can be held accountable for their work by any reasonable professional standard. These institutions provided an environment that enabled the benefits of education to permeate the lives of previously enslaved people.

Educational institutions play a crucial role in shaping the community and are expected to produce specific results and benefits, such as higher literacy rates and educational attainment among community members. They are tasked with creating a well-educated workforce that attracts businesses and fosters economic development within the community.

Education fosters understanding, tolerance, and cooperation among diverse community members. Educated community members are likely to participate in civic activities such as voting, volunteering, promoting healthier lifestyles, and maintaining access to healthcare information.

Higher education levels are associated with lower crime rates, and educational institutions often serve as cultural hubs that offer a range of arts, music, and cultural events. Education encourages innovation and creativity, leading to new ideas and solutions for community challenges.

Educated communities are more likely to engage in sustainable practices and environmental conservation, support family stability, and improve parenting skills. These outcomes contribute to the overall well-being and prosperity of the community, creating a positive and supportive environment for all its members.

HBCUs are the only institutions that took on the responsibility to provide the benefits of education to the previously enslaved Black community. The HBCU tradition began before the Civil War and continued afterward, driven by the Black population's understanding of the benefits of education. Free Blacks were prohibited from participating in the existing educational system, and those who were enslaved were prohibited by law.

Missionary and church groups established underground networks to assist runaways settling in the North, but governments provided no official action. Missionary abolitionist groups, such as the American Anti-Slavery Society, offered financial assistance to advocate against slavery as a moral issue using lectures, newspapers, and pamphlets. Political abolitionists advocated against the spread of slavery beyond the states where it was legally allowed and used politics to achieve their goals.

From its inception, the delivery of education to the community was not the responsibility of the governmental authority with control over the community. Whether or not education was provided depended on the knowledge within a family unit and the family's financial capability to afford the cost of education.

The intrinsic value of education and its external benefits led various institutions to start providing education beyond the family, which spread to benefit the community. Many early schools were established and run by religious institutions, providing basic education and moral instruction.

Towns or groups of parents often organize local schools to educate children in their communities. They set up tuition-based schools to offer education to those who could contribute, with the assistance of traveling schoolmasters.

Women ran small schools in their homes, teaching basic literacy and numeracy to young children. Some families hired private tutors or educated their children at home, while wealthier families sent their children to boarding schools, which provided a more comprehensive education.

Churches or benevolent societies ran charity schools for poor children, ensuring they received some education. Enrolling children in apprenticeships provided practical training and rudimentary instruction in reading, writing, and arithmetic.

These practices laid the foundation for the elementary and secondary education system we recognize as an integral part of our communities, evolving to meet society's changing needs. These educational systems started before the Civil War but were not available to the Black population, enslaved or free.

HBCUs were the exclusive education providers before and after the Civil War, and they were joined by the Union Army, with the assistance of missionary groups and the Freedmen Bureau, as institutions providing education to the Black community after the war. Therefore, the HBCU educational network is responsible for addressing the academic needs of Black communities and any gaps in performance between Black and the U.S. populations.

HBCUs are responsible for eliminating the literacy and civil rights gaps and reducing the size of the economic gap between the Black and the U.S. populations. These accomplishments were the byproduct of HBCUs achieving their primary mission: to educate the Black community.

However, to close the economic gap, HBCUs must address the performance gap between the Black and U.S. college-age populations, as well as the performance gap between HBCUs and the U.S. college retention and graduation rates.

Closing the performance gaps between these academic activities will directly address the most outstanding components of the economic gap. One of the leading sources of the economic gap shown in Figure 7.3 is the difference in median annual wage rates between the Black and the U.S. labor forces.

Data from the Bureau of Labor Statistics for 2024 show that the median annual wage is approximately 44 percent, or $20,000, lower for Black workers than for the U.S. labor force. One of the leading forces driving the size of the gap in annual wages is Black workers' overrepresentation in low-wage jobs and underrepresentation in higher-wage jobs.

For example, although the Black population represents around 13 percent of the U.S. population, it accounts for more than 35 percent of all nursing assistants in the United States. This represents overrepresentation in low-wage jobs, especially compared to the 6 percent of Black workers who are registered nurses and the 4 percent who are physicians, and underrepresentation in high-wage jobs.

Occupational Employment and Wage Statistics from the Bureau of Labor Statistics show the average annual salary for nurse assistants, registered nurses (RNs), and physicians. These data track the difference between low-skill, low-wage jobs and high-skill, high-wage jobs in every industry.

In the health industry, nurse assistants earn $39,610, RNs earn $89,010, and physicians earn $239,200. Physicians typically earn significantly more than registered nurses, who earn more than nurse assistants. Converting nurse assistants into registered nurses and physicians is directly related to the amount of education and training each worker receives during their lifetime.

This difference in wages is due to the varying levels of education, training, and responsibilities required for each role. High-wage jobs are typically high-skill positions that require more advanced educational preparation; therefore, enhancing the performance of the HBCU educational network in attracting students plays a crucial role in narrowing the economic gap.

Increasing the percentage of the Black college-age population enrolled to the same or higher level as the U.S. college-age population, shown in Figure 7.4, would create more Black students to pursue high-skill, high-wage jobs. Because HBCUs enroll a higher percentage of Black students, efforts to improve their enrollment would significantly impact reaching or exceeding the U.S. percentage of the college-age population enrolled.

Figure 7.4 illustrates a notable increase in enrollment among the college-age population of the United States during the early 1970s, which coincided with the passage of the Great Society legislation in 1965. Title IV of the Higher Education Act of 1965 established several financial aid methods, including loans, designed to provide students with the necessary funding to cover the cost of college.

The funding is provided exclusively to students attending a postsecondary educational institution in the United States. It helps cover the many costs associated with postsecondary education and is available from federal and state governments, academic institutions, and private organizations. It can be awarded through grants, loans, work-study programs, and scholarships.

Students must first complete the Free Application for Federal Student Aid (FAFSA) to apply for federal financial aid. This part of the financial assistance program provides enrollment management, whereby students are awarded money based on merit, need, and the students families' financial status.

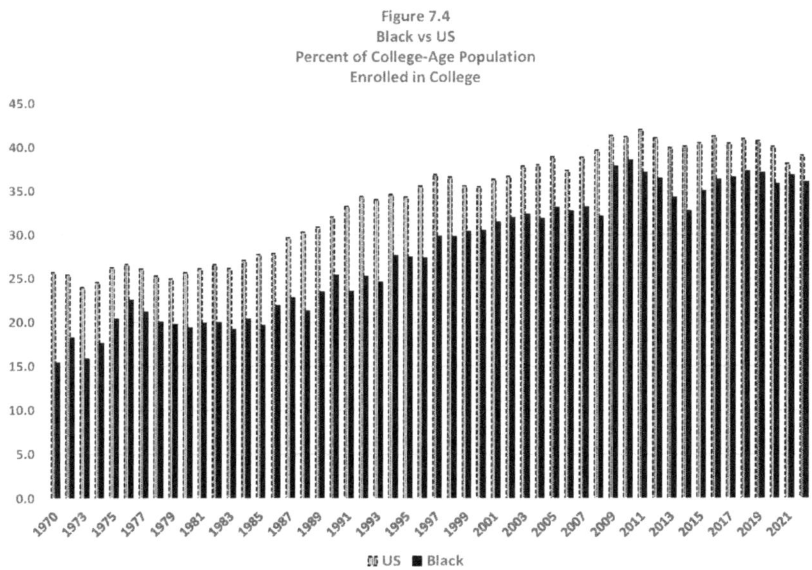

FIGURE 7.4 Black versus U.S. percent of college-age population enrolled in college

Figure 7.4 illustrates a steeper increase in enrollment for the Black college-age population compared to the U.S. college-age population during the early 1970s. Eventually, the 10-point gap between the two in 1970 narrowed to a 3-point gap by 2022, demonstrating the effectiveness of the federal college financial aid options in increasing Black college enrollment.

This college financial aid program is partly attributable to the contributions of the HBCU student nonviolent revolutionaries to the Civil Rights Movement, which prompted the passage of the Great Society legislation. Therefore, it represents another notable achievement by HBCUs that has a significant positive impact on the enrollment of the Black college-age population.

Still, a gap exists in enrollment rates between the overall U.S. and Black college-age populations, as several factors, beyond financial, contribute to this disparity. While student loans help many students afford college, concerns about debt can deter some Black students from using loans to attend college.

Black families, on average, have lower household incomes and less wealth than U.S. families and are unfamiliar with college financial aid opportunities. This economic disparity makes it more challenging for Black students to afford college, even with the availability of financial options, including loans.

HBCUs and other institutions serving a higher percentage of Black students may have fewer resources than PWIs, which can impact the quality of educational support services available and lead to disparities in access to information about financial aid and college planning resources. For these and other reasons, Black students might not receive the same guidance and support in navigating the college application and financial aid processes.

In addition, unequal access to quality K-12 education may contribute to the college enrollment gap. Next to the financial cost associated with attending college, the greatest obstacle is the lack of basic common-sense information regarding the economic advantages of obtaining a postsecondary education.

Ultimately, there are legal incentives in the United States for parents to provide their children with a secondary education. After the expiration of the legal incentive, there is no remaining incentive to obtain postsecondary training unless there is knowledge within the household that understands the relationship between high-skill, high-wage, and low-skill, low-wage jobs.

Closing the economic gap by addressing the enrollment gap requires an approach that tackles these and many other underlying issues. However, exceeding the enrollment rate gap for the U.S. college-age population is not impossible because Black female students, as shown in Figure 7.5, have already achieved this.

Figures 7.4 and 7.5 both show a positive trend toward a larger portion of the college-age population deciding to obtain some form of postsecondary educational training. This trend is enhanced by the availability of financial aid programs and technology that provides more flexible and affordable options for students seeking educational training.

Once again, HBCUs find themselves in an ideal position to close another one of the gaps the Black population has faced since acquiring freedom by running from enslavement to the Union Army lines. The task is to enlist the Black college-age population in a competition to exceed the enrollment percentage of the U.S. college-age population, which Black females have achieved.

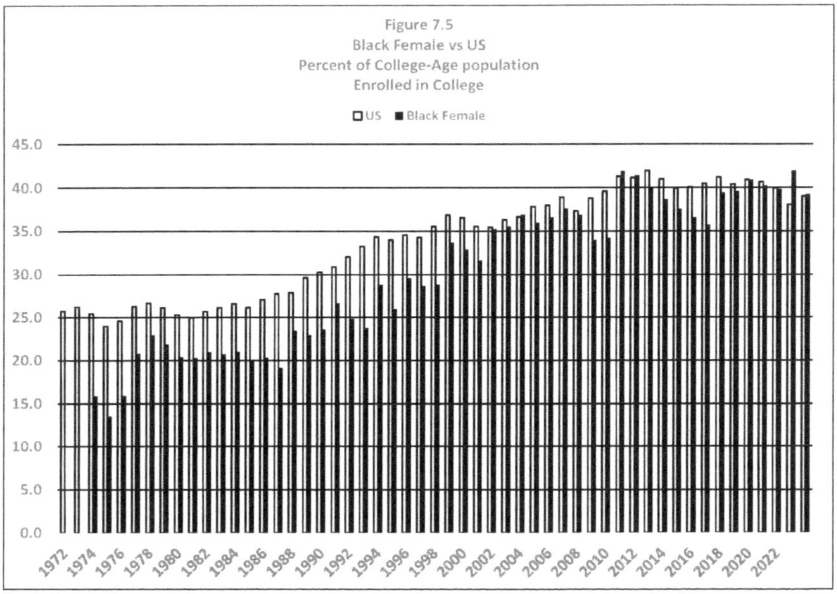

FIGURE 7.5 Black female versus U.S. percent of college-age population enrolled in college

The performance of the Black female college-age population indicates that eliminating this enrollment gap can be achieved and exceeded. The challenge is for each HBCU to devise and execute an internal strategy to increase enrollment, review and revise the approach, and share any successful approach with the HBCU educational network. This iterative process should lead to the enrollment levels achieved among the Black female college-age populations.

Attracting more students to the campuses of HBCUs to address the enrollment gap associated with the percentage of the Black college-age population enrolled in college is only one of three gaps to be closed in the HBCU effort to close the economic gap.

7.4 The Retention Gap

Enrollment, retention, and graduation are the three performance gaps that must be closed on the path to closing the economic gap. Currently, this is the last task before HBCUs can complete their primary mission. Figure 7.6 shows the gap between HBCU and U.S. college retention rates.

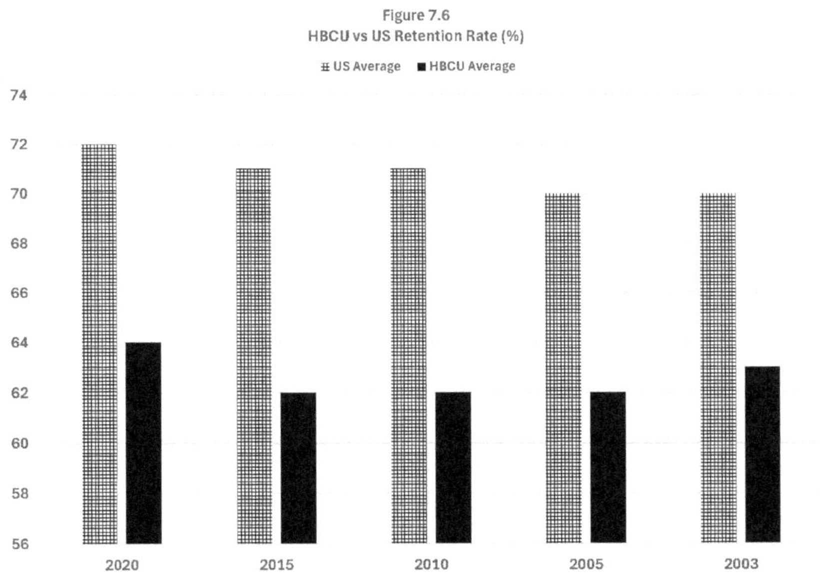

FIGURE 7.6 HBCU versus U.S. retention rate (percent)

The college retention rates represent the percentage of first-time, full-time degree- and certificate-seeking undergraduate students who return in the fall of the given year. The data are from the U.S. Department of Education's Integrated Postsecondary Education Data System (IPEDS).

The college retention rate refers to the percentage of students who continue their studies at the same institution from one academic year to the next. It is a key indicator of student satisfaction, academic success, and the effectiveness of the institution's support services.

High retention rates indicate that students are engaged, supported, and making good progress in their studies. In contrast, low retention rates may indicate academic difficulties, financial challenges, or dissatisfaction with the institution.

The data in Figure 7.6 represent the average retention rates for all U.S. colleges compared to those for HBCUs. For the years covered, the HBCU retention rate has been 7.3 points lower than the rate of U.S. colleges.

Closing this retention gap is another critical step toward narrowing the growing economic gap between the Black population and the U.S. population, as educational attainment is a key factor in determining whether workers secure high-skill, high-wage jobs or low-skill, low-wage jobs.

Creating an appealing campus environment is positively correlated with higher retention rates, which are positively correlated with higher educational attainment, which is a key factor in closing the economic gap. Therefore, HBCUs' primary mission now includes creating such an environment.

This was not one of the original tasks HBCUs needed to perform to achieve their primary mission. In the beginning, HBCU students only had one option regarding educational attainment: an HBCU.

When HBCU students' efforts led to closing the civil rights gap, new enrollment opportunities opened up for the Black college-age population. HBCUs were now required to create an appealing campus environment that could compete against PWIs for what used to be the traditional students and exclusive customers of the HBCUs.

The first step to creating an appealing campus environment capable of competing against PWIs is analyzing information obtained from the 64 percent of students that Figure 7.6 shows HBCUs were able to retain. This analysis can provide information that HBCUs could use to attract and retain a larger percentage of their students. The information can be evaluated, revised, and shared until and after the HBCU retention rates equal or exceed the U.S. rate.

7.5 The Graduation Gap

Improving the retention rate is required before improving graduation rates. The college graduation rate refers to the percentage of students who complete their degree programs within a specified period, typically within four to six years for a bachelor's degree.

This metric assesses an institution's effectiveness in supporting students through the completion of their studies. High graduation rates indicate that many students are successfully earning their degrees. In contrast, low graduation rates may indicate challenges in retention, academic support, or other factors that affect student success.

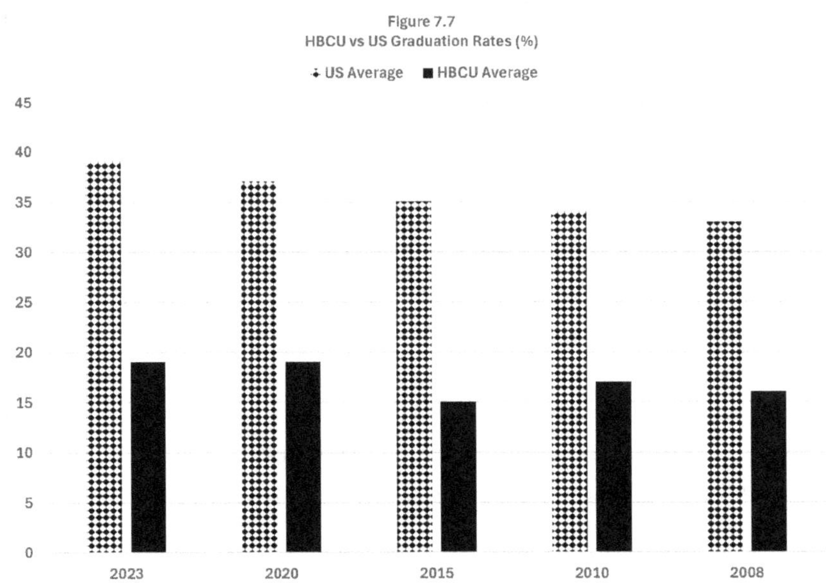

FIGURE 7.7 HBCU versus U.S. graduation rates (percent)

Figure 7.7 illustrates a graduation rate gap by comparing the averages of 4-year graduation rates for bachelor's degrees within 100 percent of the expected time for HBCUs and all U.S. higher education institutions over several years. This measure refers to the percentage of students who complete their bachelor's degree within four years, which is considered the standard or typical time frame for completing such a degree.

This metric evaluates an institution's efficiency and effectiveness in helping students graduate on time. A higher four-year graduation rate indicates that a larger proportion of students can complete their degree programs within the expected time frame, reflecting positively on the institution's support services, academic programs, and overall student success.

Strategies designed to improve graduation rates must address several factors contributing to lower college graduation rates. For example, many students face financial difficulties that can lead to dropping out.

High tuition costs, lack of financial aid, and the need to work while studying can all impact a student's ability to complete their degree. First-generation college students, students from low-income backgrounds, and underrepresented minorities often face these and additional challenges that can affect their graduation rates.

Some students who are not adequately prepared for college-level coursework may struggle academically, leading to lower retention and graduation rates. Quality support services, such as academic advising, tutoring, and mental health services, may not be readily available; however, they play a crucial role in student success.

Institutions with robust support systems that foster a sense of connection among students and their campus community, as well as engagement in extracurricular activities, tend to have higher graduation rates. Engaged students are more likely to persist and graduate, whereas a lack of engagement can lead to feelings of isolation and increased dropout rates.

Balancing personal and family responsibilities with academic demands can be challenging for many students, particularly those who are parents or caregivers. Physical and mental health problems can significantly impact a student's ability to stay in school and complete their degree.

The research identifying these factors as contributors to lower graduation rates suggests that addressing them requires a comprehensive approach. Before establishing priorities, HBCUs must determine the connection between financial support, academic preparation, robust support services, and community engagement efforts. In addition, retention rates must be included in any strategy designed to improve graduation rates, as the same factors impact both rates.

Figure 7.7 shows that the graduation rates for all U.S. institutions are slightly less than 40 percent, while the rates for HBCUs hover slightly below 20 percent. These rates suggest that it is challenging to guide a student from their freshman year to graduation, with 4 out of 10 students achieving this goal by the former, compared to 2 out of 10 for the latter.

However, some HBCUs regularly achieve graduation rates above 50 percent. These HBCUs belong to an unofficial group called the Black Ivy League, representing about seven HBCUs, depending on who counts.

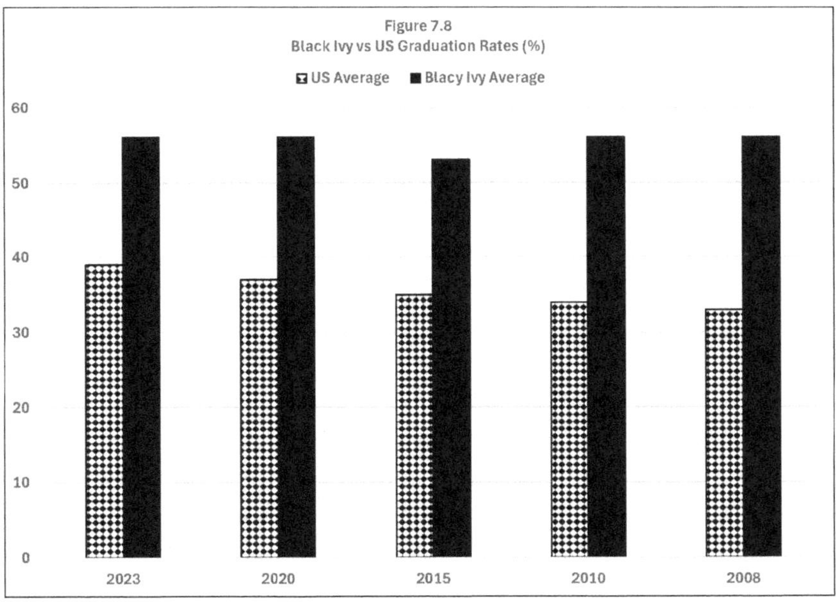

FIGURE 7.8 Black Ivy versus U.S. graduation rates (percent)

Figure 7.8 uses Department of Education IPEDS data to compare the graduation rate for the Black Ivy League to all U.S. institutions. For all the years shown, the

Black Ivy League graduation rates have exceeded the U.S. rate and consistently hovered above 50 percent, a target for all HBCUs.

Such an effort would go a long way toward narrowing the economic gap, the last task required before HBCUs achieve their principal mission. Providing the Black community with the education required to compete for survival on the same level as every citizen is the last battle in the war HBCUs were created to fight and win.

Conclusion

The current popularity of HBCUs is directly connected to the death of Richard Humphreys, a Quaker philanthropist who left in his will a sum of $10,000 to fund the construction of a future school dedicated to the "descendants of the African Race." On February 25, 1837, a group of Philadelphians used this financial gift to start the Institute for Colored Youth, which later became Cheyney University of Pennsylvania and is the nation's oldest HBCU.

When people unite for a positive, worthy purpose, such as passing on knowledge, their actions create a ripple effect, similar to the ripples formed by tossing a stone into a still pond. Although imperceptible to human eyes, each ripple will ultimately reach the shore.

Today's popularity of HBCUs is one of those ripples reaching the shore, created by that initial positive step of providing education to the Black community. Since then, those who have devoted their lives to developing the HBCU educational network have continually thrown stones into the pond. The ripples returning to the shores come in all shapes and sizes. Today, they manifest as social media tidal waves or tsunamis, encouraging enrollment in HBCUs among the college-age population.

The popularity stems from the Black community's understanding that HBCUs have supported them all along and still stand as the only physical institutions in America dedicated to enhancing Black lives and carving out a place for them in America's democracy. After exploring other solutions, the Black community acknowledges the unique role that the HBCU educational network has played in the economic and cultural development of the Black community and the ongoing work it must accomplish.

Any changes in the popularity of attending HBCUs or choosing to live in a predominantly Black community among Black Americans are understandable. The grass is always perceived to be greener on the other side, so the Black community integrated into mainstream American society once it was given the opportunity.

The opportunities gained from the success of the Civil Rights Movement, manifested in access to better schools, jobs, and homes, often lay outside the traditional Black community and were too tempting to ignore. They were earned and long overdue. Overall, the Black community has benefited from seizing these opportunities—advantages that can be measured in terms of higher household incomes, increased educational attainment levels, and enhanced overall economic mobility.

Despite enjoying the cultural and economic benefits of being part of the traditional Black community, the best and brightest families moved out of the neighborhood in search of greener pastures. The unintended collateral damage of these departures was a decline in the economic performance of the traditional Black community.

The departure of higher-income households lowered the median household income of the remaining families in the traditional Black community census tract. It is difficult for census tracts with lower-than-average household incomes to attract the retail and commercial private sector investments required to attract higher-income households as residents.

As a result, as the economic performance of traditional Black communities began to decline, HBCUs that were in these communities and relied on them for support for their students, faculty, and staff were adversely affected. HBCUs and the traditional Black community maintained a symbiotic relationship, where the institutions' activities created economic mobility and opportunities for the community.

However, after the success of the Civil Rights Movement, more significant opportunities emerged beyond the traditional Black community. HBCUs were now required to compete against the advantages that integration into American society provided to the Black community for the resources they needed to survive.

As Black families changed their decisions about living in traditional Black communities, they also revised their choices about where to send their children to college, resulting in a severe drop in the HBCU market share of Black college student enrollment, from 90 percent to 10 percent. However, the economic health of HBCUs remained relatively sound despite the loss of market share because the success of the Civil Rights Movement expanded the market size, as a larger percentage of the Black college-age population could afford and chose to attend college.

Therefore, the economic fate of the traditional Black community depends on the ongoing success of HBCUs and their efforts to promote economic growth. The resurgence of HBCUs is essential to enhance the economic mobility of the traditional Black community to a level comparable to that of the average community in the United States.

The HBCU educational network was responsible for the economic mobility of the Black population after they escaped from slavery by fleeing the plantations to fight for their freedom. The strategic planning utilized by HBCUs to enhance their business model will help close the academic performance gaps and boost the economic mobility necessary to bridge the financial divide between the traditional Black community and the average U.S. community and return HBCUs to their principal mission.

Bibliography

Beckert, Sven. *Empire of cotton: A global history*. Vintage, 2015.

Blight, David W. *Frederick Douglass: prophet of freedom*. Simon and Schuster, 2018.

Blow, Charles M. "The devil you know: A black power manifesto." 2021.

Building Communities From the Inside Out: A Path Toward Finding and Mobilizing a Community's Assets, by John P. Kretzmann and John L. McKnight.

DuBois, William Edward Burghardt. *The education of Black people: Ten critiques, 1906-1960*. NYU Press, 2001.

Ellison, Ralph, and Joe Morton. *Invisible man*. New York: Random House, 1952.

Favors, Jelani M. *Shelter in a time of storm: How Black colleges fostered generations of leadership and activism*. UNC Press Books, 2019.

Foner, Eric. "Reconstruction: America's unfinished revolution, 1863-1877." 1988.

Frazier, Franklin. "Black Bourgeoisie: The Rise of a New Middle Class in the United States." (1957): 44-46.

Harris, Adam. "The State Must Provide: Why America's Colleges Have Always Been Unequal—And How To Set Them Right by Adam Harris." *The Review of Higher Education* 45, no. 4 (2022): 565-567.

Joseph, Peniel E. *The third reconstruction: America's struggle for racial justice in the twenty-first century*. Hachette UK, 2022.

King Jr, Martin Luther. *Why we can't wait*. Penguin, 2000.

Lovett, B. L. *America's historically black colleges and universities: A narrative history for the nineteenth century into the twenty-first century*. Mercer University Press, 2015.

Myrdal, Gunnar. *An American Dilemma: The Negro Problem and Modern Democracy, Volume 1*. Routledge, 2017.

Stodghill, Ron. *Where Everybody Looks Like Me: At the Crossroads of America's Black Colleges and Culture*. Vol. 22. Amistad, 2015.

Wilkerson, Isabel. *The warmth of other suns: The epic story of America's great migration*. Penguin UK, 2020.

Williams, Eric. "Capitalism and slavery." In *Sociological Worlds*, pp. 260-268. Routledge, 2013.

Woodson, Carter Godwin. *The Negro in our history*. Associated Publishers, 1922.

www.ingramcontent.com/pod-product-compliance
Lightning Source LLC
LaVergne TN
LVHW082338200926
848481LV00012B/3377
9798385188925